FROM THE HEART OF IRELAND

BRENDAN POWER was born in Fethard-on-Sea in County Wexford but now lives in the north of England. He is a founder and past president of the Professional Speakers' Association of Europe and is recognised as one of Europe's leading motivational speakers. His unique style, intriguingly described by one client as 'dynamic laid back', has made him popular with major companies and organisations on four continents.

Brendan spent ten years in broadcasting in the UK and the Caribbean and a number of years in sales, where he was described as being in the top 2 per cent of salespeople in the UK. For more information see www.BrendanPower.com

FROM THE HEART
OF IRELAND

COMPILED BY BRENDAN POWER

A Brandon Original Paperback
First published in 2003 by
Brandon
an imprint of Mount Eagle Publications
Unit 3 Olympia Trading Estate, Coburg Road, London N22 6TZ, England
and Dingle, Co. Kerry, Ireland

ISBN 0 86322 316 8

10 9 8 7 6 5 4 3 2 1

Illustrations on pages i, 72, 159, 178, 206
© 2003 Raymond Foley
Celtic Illustrations © 1996–2002, Cari Buziak.
www.Aon-Celtic.com. All rights reserved.

Cover photograph: Steve MacDonogh
Cover design: id communications
Typesetting: Red Barn Publishing, Skibbereen
Printed by the Woodprintcraft Group Ltd, Dublin

For
Sebastian
and, of course, for
Laura
and her sister Andrea

Contents

Introduction

WELCOME TO *The Heart of Ireland.* In general, you will be reading this for one of two reasons – either you have already bought the book or you are thinking about buying it.

If you already own it, there are two ways to enjoy it, and if you are a prospective owner, there are two reasons why you should go ahead and buy it.

The two ways to enjoy it: firstly, you could, of course, read it like most books – start at the beginning and work your way through to the end – and if that's what you want to do, that's fine, and I know you will enjoy it. Alternatively, you can just open it anywhere at random and be inspired by whatever story faces you. It has been compiled in such a way that whenever you have got a few minutes to spare – even while the commercials are interrupting your favourite TV programme – you can read a full story, or two. You can just dip in and out whenever the mood takes you and in just a few minutes gain inspiration from one of the many stories.

Now, two reasons why I believe you should buy it. Number one is for the two reasons above – it is a great read at any time of the day. Number two is that you will be helping a great cause – Laura's Hope (you will find more details of this at the back of the book).

I would like to take the opportunity to thank a few people for their help and support in making this book possible. First on that list are the contributors – not the ones whose stories you can read here, but those who submitted stories and didn't make the final selection. Those people provided their time, their talent and their support for the project but then missed out on the pleasure of seeing their stories in print. I enjoyed reading every story I received, and deselecting some of them was one of the most difficult things I have ever had to do. Secondly, thank you to all those who are included in the book; your support is also very much appreciated.

Before I started on this book, I expected to end up with a favourite story, but now that it's finished, I haven't. Reading, and rereading, all the stories allowed me to experience all the emotions imaginable. I laughed at some and cried at others; I shared the pain of some and the love of others. Although some of our writers are successful professionals and others are being published for the first time, it is impossible for me to pick a favourite; they all have something special to offer.

One person in particular I would like to thank is Sean Lyons of Tralee. Sean put in a tremendous amount of work behind the scenes – and even made the ultimate sacrifice by putting me up in his house when I was in Kerry!

And finally, there is one other person to mention, someone who provides me with unlimited enthusiasm, not just for this book, but for everything! He can't read this yet – but he will one day. My grandson, Sebastian Power.

Brendan Power
July 2003

The Mahogany Seat

Mary Arrigan

'LOT NUMBER 127, a fine mahogany lavatory seat. Beautifully hand turned.'

A wave of sniggering swept around the crowded room as the auctioneer's assistant held up the seat, his comical face framed in the hole. Smarmy twit. But then, he didn't know its story.

I was nine years old the year I went to stay with Cassie and Pa Hayes. Cassie had worked for years in Mum's old home, so when she heard that I'd had pneumonia, she insisted that I come to her for a bit of TLC and fresh air.

'A couple of weeks of country air and old Cassie's cooking and you'll be fat and rosy,' she said, smothering me in her plump arms. 'I don't do fat and rosy!' I wanted to shout, angry at being dumped late at night in a sleepy time warp with two old fogeys.

Clucking hens and Pa shouting to the postman drifted into my early morning dreaming. Before donning my sorrowful, put-upon face, I needed to go to the loo. Downstairs Cassie was baking bread, her round face beaming goodwill at me. I hoped she wasn't going to suffocate me in those arms again.

'Cassie,' I began, red-faced and cross-legged. 'Please, where's the toilet?'

'The lav is it, sweetheart?' she laughed. 'You poor child, you must be dying to go.'

She led me across the yard. 'There.' She pointed to a tiny wooden building. 'Go on now, and I'll be putting on your breakfast.'

The relief on reaching the ramshackle loo quickly dissolved when I saw the long wooden seat with the hole in the middle and heard the buzzing flies. I told God he'd done enough damage already by allowing me to be abandoned here on this lonely farm, so why did he have to inflict this smelly hut on me and my full bladder?

The stone floor had recently been swilled out with disinfectant, which had settled in small puddles on the uneven surface. Squares of newspaper hung on a nail, faces in photographs oblivious of their future function. No amount of desperation was going to get me into that place. Glancing around for any sign of Pa, I ran behind a stone wall to a spot where there were no nettles.

Cassie turned on her bright beam again when I got back to the kitchen. 'You must be starved, alannah,' she said, turning eggs in the pan. 'Wait till you get a taste of this home-cured bacon.'

Scrumptious. But on principle I left some on my plate.

Pa's entrance through the squeaky back door brought the faint whiff of disinfectant. More than ever I wanted to go home.

'Come with me to look for eggs, alannah,' said Cassie. 'Some of the old hens are laying in the ditches, the daft things.'

That sounded like a fun idea, but then I remembered the misery bit.

'No, I'd prefer to read,' I said grandly. 'Have you any books?' I was satisfied when I saw the perplexed look on Pa's face.

'There are some in the parlour,' Cassie said as she scraped my carefully left scraps into the hen bucket. 'Suit yourself, alannah.' She had called my bluff.

The over-furnished parlour smelled of furniture cream and damp. A stuffed fox looked glassily at me as I wandered around, touching the china ornaments. The walls were hung with sentimental Victorian prints of children praying and dogs mourning dead masters. This wasn't a people-room; it was a dreary museum. I swallowed my pride and ran to catch up with Cassie. We found sixteen eggs.

That evening, after supper, Pa invited me into his wood-workshop, a wonderland of carved figures and smooth reliefs.

'Wow,' I whispered, forgetting to be a martyr. 'They're great.'

Pa watched me with pride as I went around to each carving in turn, running my fingers lightly over them. Pa identified all the bits of wood that lay waiting to be turned into living creatures.

'Look at the colours in that,' he said, holding a big chunk of dark wood. 'This is my prized possession. This is mahogany. I'm saving this for something special.' He fondled it lovingly before replacing it on the shelf. Then he handed me a small carved cat. 'For you,' he said.

'Oh, I couldn't,' I began, partly from politeness, but mostly because I realised that, if I took it, I could no longer show resentment at being in his house. It was a measure of the man's talent that I couldn't resist that little cat.

The next morning it rained. I dashed across the yard only to find that my spot behind the wall was submerged in mud and water. The thick mud squelched over my sandals and between my toes. When I got back, soaking wet and thoroughly miserable, I slopped angrily into the kitchen. Cassie recoiled at this wet, raging thing.

'Alannah, you're soaking wet,' she cried, her plump face wobbling with concern.

'Of course, I'm wet,' I raged. 'And my name is not alannah. And I can't use that stupid old loo.' I pointed towards the yard. 'And I hate this place and I hate my parents for leaving me here and I hate . . .' I looked at Cassie's anxious face and all my emotions boiled over in a blubbering mess.

'You poor little thing,' cooed Cassie, smothering me in those big arms. 'There, there.' She dried my tears with a tea towel that smelled of fried rashers. To her great credit, Cassie had the vision to see me as a small nine-year-old in strange surroundings and not as the tedious horror I was trying to be.

'Of course, you can't use that old place,' she said. 'Now, don't worry. We'll sort it out.'

After breakfast, without leaving scraps, I played in my room with the wooden cat. I could hear the mumble of conversation below. I hoped Cassie wasn't discussing my predicament with Pa. I couldn't bear for him, who magicked life into hunks of wood, to know that I had bodily functions.

Later, Cassie called me downstairs. She had two buckets, one filled with hot water, the other with cold. In her pocket she had a packet of soap-powder and a scrubbing brush.

'Take that bucket of cold water,' she said, 'alannah.'

'Where are we going?' I asked, curious and suspicious.

'Just follow me,' replied Cassie.

We slopped down the avenue to a derelict house behind some trees across the lane.

'Smythes – with a Y,' said Cassie. 'The last of them sold off the land and emigrated to some place where there's sunshine and heavy traffic.'

'But why are we . . . ?' I began.

'Shush. Trust old Cassie.'

We had reached a small building at the rear of the house. Cassie eased open the door.

'There,' she said triumphantly. Mounted regally on a raised platform stood a magnificent porcelain WC. Overhead was a cast-iron cistern with a chain from which hung an enamel art-nouveau handle with blue designs faded by generations of Smythe-with-a-Y hands. 'Madam's private privy.'

Well, I had to laugh. Together we chatted as we stripped away the grime of years. As a dramatic finale, Cassie stood on the WC and emptied the bucket of cold water into the cistern.

'There,' she puffed as she stepped down. 'Water's been cut off for years, so we'll fill that cistern every morning, and you can flush it every evening.' Her eyes shone with pride. How could I not respond positively? But I was nine years old and the world existed only for me.

'It hasn't got a seat,' I said.

Cassie's eyes clouded for just a moment. 'A seat is it?' she laughed, wiping perspiration from her upper lip with the back of her wrist. 'Well, let's look for one.'

We searched around the outbuildings, disturbing scurrying creatures and sending the raggedy crows wheeling overhead. When she realised our search was fruitless, Cassie sat down heavily on a tree stump, deflated and defeated. On my account, I tentatively put my hand on her shoulder.

'It doesn't matter, Cassie,' I said. 'The lav's great.'

She swung around and once more engulfed me in those soft arms. I didn't mind. Now that my battlefront had crumbled, I felt safe and comfortable and, above all, loved in spite of myself. I held her hand all the way back.

Cassie called me late the next morning. 'You were in such a sound sleep I hadn't the heart to waken you,' she laughed.

'Don't go looking for the eggs until I come back,' I shouted as I crossed the lane.

When I got to my exclusive loo, I laughed out loud. On the porcelain WC was a magnificent wooden seat. Although it had been sanded to a skin-smooth finish, I recognised Pa's piece of precious mahogany.

When I breathlessly ran back later to thank him, he just ruffled my hair and laughed.

'But, Pa,' I said, 'you were saving that for a special occasion.'

'You're my special occasion,' he said, winking over at Cassie.

I spent the rest of that idyllic summer cocooned in the earthy affection of Cassie and Pa. When I was thrust, shiny-shoed and Sunday-frocked, into the back of my parents' car, Pa leaned in through the window.

'Your special mahogany seat will always hang in my workshop, waiting for your next visit,' he whispered.

I never did get to see Cassie and Pa again. We moved around, and my letters to them gradually fizzled out. Cassie died, and now Pa was gone, too. An obscure relative had decided to put the house and contents up for auction – the lifetime gatherings of two gentle people fragmented into labelled lots. Two gentle people who found a core of goodness in a small, waspish girl all those years ago.

With jaw-clenching determination, I looked up at the auctioneer and prepared to outbid all others for my mahogany seat.

A Personal Journey – to Hell and Back

Frances Gaynor

T HE CLOCK BESIDE me says 10 a.m. and reluctantly I slide
gingerly out of bed from my night sitting position.
Despite two recent hip replacements, my back has now suc-
cumbed to osteoarthritis, and for the first half hour out of
bed I manoeuvre around the bedroom in a bent over position
holding on to the furniture. I turn on the radio and the opening music of *The Pat Kenny Show* is heard. It's a fine morning and I feel good.

I have been in Galway now for six weeks. The change
from home in Bagenalstown has been well worth the hassle
of finding a flat and negotiating all the roundabouts of the
city's traffic. I have not managed to find a job that suits me,
however, so I am returning home next week, but I'm glad I
came here.

I have seen the thunderous Atlantic waves break off the
rocks as I've gazed from the top of Dun Aengus in
Inishmore. I've traversed every nook and cranny of the city
on foot, seen *Antigone* at the Town Hall Theatre and hope
to see The Druid's production of *The Good Father*.

I am doing a course at GMIT, and best of all, I have spent
innumerable hours in bookshops and coffee houses as well
as seeing all the 'big' pictures at the Omniplex.

I have borderline personality disorder – BPD for short –
an illness characterised by depression, feelings of alienation,

paranoia and hopelessness. Thankfully, these days, I have the illness only intermittently, because, you see, now I can cope.

Many disparate theories have been postulated for the onset of BPD, ranging from childhood abuse to faulty genes. I had a, generally, happy childhood with parents who loved and encouraged me, so it certainly wasn't that. Yet, at age thirty-nine I fell apart.

I have never been the same since. I can be impulsive, unstable and angry – what anger! But I can also be perceptive, loving and empathetic.

I have taken several overdoses and been hospitalised on countless occasions. The 'down' is a pit with serpents, or a coffin in the ground with the lid on and no one to call. The 'up' is travelling on trains and planes, chatting with friends and my beloved books.

The turning point in my recovery happened when I met a caring doctor who accepted me as I was and who helped me build a bridge from darkness and despair to a place of hope and brightness. Her faith in me, combined with daily medication, has made life worthwhile again.

Since retiring from active nursing in 1997, peace is to be found in my little house in County Carlow, my old car, my neighbour, who is a wise woman, and my family and friends. I have not overdosed for five years and have not been in hospital for four and a half.

When the demons come, I take my car and go up the hills around my home, listening to the little streams rushing down through the heather, or I put on some Bach or Beethoven until I find myself again. In other words, I now take control of the situation rather than letting the situation control me.

I have seen many places and have explored the deep recesses of my mind. Once, I did not like myself very much and worried about the future, but lately I have come to realise that each day looks after itself.

Like today. I am sitting, relaxing, in Carraroe with a copy

of *Galway Now* before me and, for the moment, not a care in the world.

In my nursing days, I once nursed a young man with Huntington's disease. His pain was palpable, as was that of his parents who loved him. He has, down the years, left a positive mark on my memory because he refused to give up. I do, too.

The Seagull

Soinbhe Lally

I'VE KNOWN ALEX for a long time. Tourists see him as the stereotypical Donegal fisherman and whip out their cameras when they see him working at his nets and lobster pots on the harbour wall. They are attracted by his grizzled beard, his weather-beaten face, the breadth and strength of his shoulders and the deep humorous chuckles that he scatters through his conversation. Afloat or ashore, Alex wears a traditional heavy-knit sweater, and on his head he sports an old bawneen cap. He has many strange tales to tell of his long years at sea but none so strange as the story of the seagull that became his friend.

Some years ago Alex spent a season fishing for lobster on the rocky south coast of Donegal Bay. Each day he set out in his half-decker fishing boat to check his pots. This was hard work because even with the help of a winch, hauling cumbersome lobster pots from the bottom of the sea is heavy work.

One day he was fishing with a net, catching bait to use in the pots. As he drew in the net, he saw that a seagull had become entangled in the meshes. He took out his knife to kill the bird because it was tearing the net in its struggle to escape. When the bird saw the knife, it shrieked in a voice that was almost human. Alex hesitated. To spare the bird he would have to cut the net. That would mean spending several hours mending it back on shore. The bird was bedraggled and half drowned. It might not even survive if he did spare it. However, he had spent too long thinking about it and could not kill it now. He reached again with his knife, cut a large hole in the net and set the bird free.

With a noisy flapping of wings, it flew to the front of the boat and perched on the gunwale. While Alex finished working with the lobster pots, it preened its dripping feathers. It was still there when he turned the boat back towards the harbour. Maybe it was shocked after its adventure, he thought, when it showed no sign of flying away. However, as the boat entered the harbour, the seabird suddenly flew off, and Alex thought he had seen the last of it.

He was mistaken. When he came to take his boat out the following day, the seagull was perched once again on the gunwale. Pleased with his new companion, Alex set off out to sea. As he checked his pots and put in new bait, the bird drew close and gobbled up scraps of fish that he threw to it. So maybe it's hungry, he thought, and fed it some more.

Day after day, the bird came to Alex's boat, always perching on the gunwale, eyeing him with its beady eyes. 'Chase it away, it's bad luck,' other fishermen said, but Alex liked the bird's company and went on feeding it fish scraps to encourage it to stay. As the weeks passed, the bird grew bolder. Often it flew right up to Alex and perched on top of his bawneen cap. The other fishermen soon grew used to the sight of Alex setting off in his boat with the seagull perched on his head, and tourists, who came to the harbour to take photographs, were thrilled to get a picture of the stereotypical fisherman with his seabird companion.

Alex's last task each day was to haul a line of lobster pots which were laid between a rocky island and jagged line of cliff several miles west of the harbour. It was a treacherous but rich fishing ground. Only an experienced fisherman would venture into the swift tidal current that ran through the channel between the island and the cliff. One August evening, as he drew near to the cliff to haul his pots, a dense sea fog rolled in suddenly from the west and closed around him in minutes. He could see nothing, neither cliffs nor island. On one side was the echoing boom of the swell flinging itself against the cliffs, and on the other side he could hear the suck of the tidal current rushing round the island.

He knew that he and his boat were in serious danger. He could search for the leader ropes to the lobster pots and try to anchor his boat to them to avoid being swept too close to the cliff, but in the dense fog there was only a chance in a million that he would find them. More likely, the boat would be lifted by the swell and dashed against the cliff face.

On the other hand, he could steer into the tidal current and make for open sea. To do that, he would have to run the gauntlet of the rocky outcroppings of the island, without being able to see them. A single mistake and his boat would be smashed in pieces on the rocks.

As Alex pondered the risks, the seagull suddenly flew up and perched on his head. 'Not now,' he said impatiently and waved it away. The bird snatched the bawneen cap from his head and disappeared into the fog. An instant later it flew back, then flew off again. Almost as if it was trying to show him the way, Alex thought. But who would trust a bird to show the way out of the predicament he was in?

The bird flew close to him once again, then turned back the way it had come. Perhaps, Alex considered, trusting the bird would be a better option than trusting to the cliff or the rocky island. He decided to follow it. Carefully, he turned the boat and went in the direction the bird had flown. Again and again the bird flew close to him, then flew forward as if to show the way. Slowly the boat drew away from the treacherous sounds of breaking swell and sucking tide and soon reached the relative safety of open sea.

Now that the boat was out of immediate danger, Alex would have been satisfied to wait an hour or two for the fog to lift before heading for harbour. He had been fogbound before and knew that the safest thing was to wait patiently for the fog to lift. However, the seagull persisted. Forward and back it flew, all the time carrying Alex's cap in its beak. It seemed determined to lead him, so he followed.

Because he had to move slowly and cautiously through the fog, the journey took a long time, but at last Alex glimpsed the high shadowy walls of the harbour looming above him and knew he was safe home. He found the entrance, and as he steered into his mooring, the seagull swooped down, dropped the cap at his feet and went back to its usual perch on the gunwale.

It was several hours more before the fog lifted and other fogbound fishing boats were able to come back to harbour. Fishermen who doubted Alex's story of how the bird led him home could not offer any alternative explanation as to how he was able to bring his boat in safely during dense fog.

Rumours of the remarkable bird spread, and locals as well as tourists came to take photographs of Alex and his seagull. I went down there myself one day and sat for an hour on the harbour wall while Alex mended a lobster pot and told me the tale of how the seagull led him safely home. 'I suppose one good turn deserves another,' he concluded with a chuckle, a chuckle that started deep inside him and spread till he shook with laughter.

'Are you telling me the truth?' I asked suspiciously.

'Why don't you ask him?' Alex replied, pointing at a large grey-winged gull that had just flown down to perch on the gunwale of his boat.

I watched Alex load his nets and his pots on to the boat. As he took his place at the wheel and started up the engine, the seagull flew up and perched on his head.

So that much I've seen with my own eyes. As for the rest, I've decided to take Alex's word for it.

The Carol Singers

Mike Harding

IT WAS ERIC Davies' idea. He was in Besse O' th' Barn Boys Brass Band and was a very good tenor horn player. I was a not bad – but not particularly good – mouth organ player.

On the day we broke up for the Christmas holidays, Eric, who had been charging down a slide we had made in the icy playground, came up to me with steaming breath and said, 'If you bring your mouth organ and I bring the tenor horn, we can go carol singing tonight.' I thought about it as one of the dinner ladies went arse over tit on the slide. 'We'll make a load of money,' he added, and in a moment of greed I said yes to what was probably my very first paid gig.

There was a small problem. My harmonica was in the key of C, and Eric's tenor horn was in the key of B Flat, which is not the basis of a good musical relationship – unless you are Stockhausen or Philip Glass. We played roughly the same tune but a full tone apart.

Of all the boys that promised to come and sing with us, only Paul Wysnevsky turned up. We did the playing and he did the singing, with me joining in when some of the parts got too hard for the mouth organ. His croaky voice wavered somewhere between the two keys, shifting from time to time into keys of his own devising. We made a lot of money that night, mostly from people who just wanted us to go away.

It was dark and cold, and snow lay on the ground, not just crisp and deep and even, but slippy and cold and wet enough to get through your boots in seconds. We must have tramped the streets for a good three or four hours knocking on doors and bursting into 'We Three Kings' or 'Good King Wenceslas' as doors opened and the light flooded out upon us.

One bemused Jewish father appeared in his dressing gown, gave us the incredible sum of ten shillings and told us to go several streets away because he was, 'on earlies and the tea pots *(tea pot lids = kids)* are in feather *(bed)*'. After the first hour the soft leather bag that Eric had brought to hold our earnings was already lumpy and fat with sixpences, half crowns, pennies and shillings.

We worked all the streets around Clarendon Road and made several pounds that night, knocking and playing and singing until our hands and feet were frozen and Paul's voice was giving out to a point where he was no longer singing but shouting in a harsh, high-pitched, tuneless bark that various dogs were taking as a threat and were responding to.

By 9 p.m. we decided to call it a night. We looked at the money; there was a lot of it. 'We shouldn't ought to keep this,' Paul said. Eric and I looked at him in amazement. 'We shouldn't make money from singing hymns. It's a sin. We should give it to the church.'

We weren't sure whether it was a sin or not, but waves of guilt fought with the onset of hypothermia, and won. So even though we were frozen half to death and had sung and played our eleven-year-old hearts out, we took a half crown each and carried the rest of the money to the presbytery. We walked quietly across the deep snow in the priests' garden, stars above us, a dog barking streets away and the noise of a steam train shunting on the far off Barney's Croft, a brick-field where last summer some tramps had burned to death trying to sleep in the brick ovens.

Monsignor Aspinall's housekeeper opened the door, and light fell on to the snow-covered lawn and us three: Eric with his shining brass horn, me with my mouth organ and Paul with the money.

'What d'yez want banging the door at this time of night?' she shouted in her Mayo accent, stamping her slippered feet on the cold, salted step.

'We've been carol singing.'

'Don't go starting with yer noise here, the Monsignor is in bed.'

'We just brought some money for the church.' She looked suspiciously at the bag in Paul's hand, and for a brief moment the thought that all small boys are not emissaries of Satan flickered across her mind.

'Yez are good lads now.' She took the bag from him.

'Happy Christmas,' we said quietly.

'And a happy Christmas to ye too. Away off home to your mothers and be careful, the roads is terrible slippy.'

We felt righteous and holy but also cold and hungry and went for a thrupenny bag of chips from the Clarendon Road chippy. We ate them under a street lamp, warming our frozen hands on the hot greasy parcels, burning our mouths on the scalding chips.

'Shall we do it again tomorrow night?' Eric asked through a mouthful of fried potatoes, lard and malt vinegar. The silence from Paul and me was enough, and as the steam from our chips ascended to the sputtering gas mantle of the lamp, the ad hoc trio of Davies, Harding and Wysnevsky broke up tacitly and without acrimony after its first and only gig.

From across the snowy streets we heard the sound of the choir from St Mark's Church of England singing 'Silent Night'. It sounded beautiful.

'That's lovely,' Eric said, 'but I bet they don't get paid as much for going away as we did.'

Cherish Change

Brendan Power

I AM SOMETHING of an enigma – a war baby born in a neutral country. I am not alone, however, for it seems that wherever we were born, if our birth took place between 1939 and 1945, we are universally known as war babies.

That also means I am in a group of survivors. Survivors of what? Well, thinking back to the world of my childhood, I would say we are survivors of half a century of change and half a century of upheaval. I suppose what I am really saying is that we have survived half a century of whatever changes life has thrown at us, and I would like to reflect on just a few of the changes we have experienced, changes that stem from a time when everybody could be gay and when political correctness simply referred to parliamentary etiquette.

Unfortunately, those days are long gone, however, and some of the changes we have encountered may seem strange and unnecessary to our generation, but no doubt some of our customs would seem equally strange and unnecessary to many of the younger generation. For instance, half a century ago it was considered normal to work for your money and pay for your goods, a concept which would be seen as almost revolutionary in these days of credit cards and credit ratings, things which for us were still far in the future, along with inflation and the Euro. We knew about money, of course; we just did not have much of it. In fact, as a child in

County Wexford, I can remember my mother many times asking me if I thought money grew on trees. Well, perhaps I did, but technology has changed all that, and today our children know that far from growing on trees, money does in fact come from a hole in the wall!

Somewhere in the dark recesses of my mind, I can still recall a time when charity was a virtue rather than an industry, and I can even remember when couples got married first and had children afterwards; the term *love child* was yet to take over from an adjective with altogether different connotations. In hindsight, they were halcyon days, days when movies were films, films were in black and white and cinemas were theatres; when radio was television and families listened together.

Cars had running boards, but no heaters. We had never heard of turbos, or GTs, or unleaded petrol; and to our simple, uncluttered, and perhaps even naive, minds, 4 × 4 was 16. It really is a never-ending list: the threshing machines of yesterday are the combine harvesters of today, that sensible gabardine rain coat has been exchanged for the ubiquitous anorak, our mothers' home cooking has been pushed aside by frozen convenience foods, and that wonderful stone slab in the pantry has been made redundant by the fridge in the fitted kitchen.

Unlike that play of yesteryear, however, I do not look back in anger, but rather with fondness, perhaps occasionally tinged with a little regret. After all, even nostalgia is not what it used to be. Some things have come, some have gone, some have come and gone and others, like paper carrier bags, have gone and come back again.

There are so many things we take for granted today, but newcomers in this past half century include such everyday items as central heating and fitted carpets, jet planes and motorways, microwaves and televisions, self-service and, lamentably, poor service. We have said goodbye to steam trains and the pony and trap, outdoor toilets and tin baths, diphtheria and TB. Immigration has taken over from emigration, the crubeen has been replaced by the hamburger, and those who were attracted by advertisements depicting the fun and camaraderie of smoking now find they were simply hastening the ultimate solitude.

We have become Europeans, and Europe is becoming a single nation, mannequins are now supermodels, sportsmen have become celebrities, amateurs have become millionaires, and criminals have become victims while their victims have become the criminals. To us it has become something of a topsy-turvy world, so perhaps it is not surprising there is a generation gap, as we get slower and the world gets faster. But, when all is said and done – and nowadays there usually is more said than done – it has been an interesting half century and definitely not one that I would have wanted to miss.

And as always the change goes on, just as the prices keep rising, but whatever the cost of living, it is still worth it, and I believe the next half century will be every bit as good as the last. This is a wonderful life, one that is here to be enjoyed, and I would certainly agree with Eleanor Roosevelt who said, 'The future belongs to those who believe in the beauty of their dreams.'

Leopold and Maria

Gerry O'Malley

LEOPOLD AND MARIA came to Ireland after the war, after four years spent in concentration camps in Germany and Italy. In the last of these, the Polish capo had said to Leopold, 'A girl from your village came in yesterday. Good looker, too.' It was Maria, to whom he had become engaged nearly six years earlier. That was before the war when they had both joined the resistance to fight fascism. They were arrested and sent to different camps. For years they didn't know of each other's whereabouts, or even whether the other was alive or dead, until that day in 1945, shortly before the war ended, when in that dreadful place, they were reunited.

Leopold is not exactly sure why he chose to come to Ireland. He had worked in his father's glass factory in Poland, but that was now in Russian hands, and he had had enough of repressive regimes.

They landed at Dún Laoghaire with very little English and even less money. They rented an attic room in Bray, and on that first day, Leopold made a rudimentary fishing line and went to the pier to catch lunch. He didn't succeed. However, their landlady was kind, and when she noticed that Maria was not in the habit of coming in laden with groceries, she began to pass gifts of food, stews, casseroles and the like, saying that they were left over from her own family dinners.

With his own hands Leopold built a small kiln, brick by brick, to make glass. He bought the materials with money he got by knocking on doors and asking to do odd jobs.

Years later the three of us would sit drinking Polish slivovitz in the drawing room of their elegant Georgian house standing in its own grounds in the most fashionable part of Bray. The beautifully proportioned room would be a-glint with candlelight on crystal, polished mahogany and soft leather. Outside the door, a large white Mercedes. The first time Leopold stood in that house was when he came to do a job on the fireplace, for which he got five shillings.

His success with the glassmaking was directly due to his choice of market. The type of glass he concentrated on was the one with the shortest life, namely, the ordinary pub glass. The demand was huge and continuous. To this day, whenever a barman or a waiter drops a tray, the crash is music in my ears, and I raise my own glass – in thought anyway – to the continued prosperity of Leopold and Maria.

Sitting with them in their luxurious house, the talk nearly always came round to their time in the camps. They would recount for each other and for me the horrors of those terrible days. The cruelties, the beatings, the cold and hunger, the ever-present threat of summary execution; things so far removed from my own experience that I could only relate to them through films I had seen. And Maria would weep quietly, which I found perfectly understandable. It was some time before I realised that she was weeping with regret for a time when survival – the very act of staying alive from one minute to the next – was a huge achievement, evidence of the indomitability of the human spirit. Nowadays, her life was so safe and secure. The biggest decision she had to make in a day was who to invite for coffee mornings.

It made me think that, maybe, after all, the Zen master got it right when he said, 'Deprivation is a blessing.'

Seize the Moment

Mary Kennedy

WE TELL OUR children we love them all the time. We reassure them when they're insecure; we convince them that no matter what happens we will never stop loving them. Why then do we find it so difficult to do the same for our parents?

I was twenty-one when my father died at the age of fifty-eight. He suffered a heart attack while playing golf. One of the horrible aspects of his going was the suddenness of it all. There was no time to say goodbye, to come to terms with this awful reality. It felt so unfair, so untimely, so shocking. I wanted to turn back the clock and relive that last morning I had seen him leave the house. If I'd known he was never coming back, I would have taken more time to chat to him over breakfast. I would have kissed and hugged him good-bye properly, not the quick peck on the cheek as he was leaving and I was rushing upstairs.

I loved him dearly and I never really told him so. I'm sure he knew I loved him, but I never said the words, 'Dad, I love you. You're a kind, gentle man and I'm lucky to have a father like you who always puts his family first, who has a wonderful sense of humour and a really laid-back approach to life.' This really bothered me for a long time after his passing, but it was too late then. However, time heals the broken heart. We pick up the pieces, and life goes on and becomes good again.

My mother was a tower of strength and support and love to me from the time my first baby was born and I began to juggle home and work life. She looked after all of my four children, and this was a great privilege for me and for them. Somehow the years passed and we got on with things, had good times and bad times. We lived, laughed and cried together, but, again, I don't ever remember actually saying those *I love you* words to my mother either. Until the last seven weeks of her life that is. Then the sadness and frustration, and sense of unfinished business I felt when my dad died so unexpectedly, came flooding back to me, and I dropped my guard and inhibitions and just loved her all the time.

She'd had a stroke and was unable to speak but was very aware of our presence at her hospital bedside. When I took her hand in mine, she'd squeeze my hand, and I felt as if my heart would burst with sheer emotion. It was a mixture of heartache and sadness and deep love for this woman who had once been so strong and in control and was now so weak and vulnerable. I told her so often during those seven weeks how much I loved her, how grateful I was for all she had done for me and for my children. I read *Little Women* to her (that was one of the stories she used to tell me at bedtime when I was very young) and I rubbed lavender scented lotion on her hands and arms. I prayed with her every evening. I lay beside her in her hospital bed and let her hair touch my face. I wanted to be physically close to her and for her to feel the love that was in my heart and in my words now for her. It was a great privilege to be able to do that.

Although life was ebbing away, there was a great sense of life and living in the moment every time I went through that hospital bedroom door. There was a beautiful, gentle, loving aura in that room for the whole seven weeks. One of the hospital chaplains, who had a great affection for Mam and prayed with her every night, told me after she died that he felt that room was a sacred place. That would have pleased her because she was a very spiritual woman who had unconditional love for her Church.

This special time of leave taking that I had with my mother was very precious, and I will treasure the memory of it always. Nonetheless, I was heartbroken when she died. A chill ran down my spine when the moment came. I felt something drain from me, right down to my toes. I wanted to reach out my hand and physically pull her back from wherever she had gone. The thoughts of her going to a place of eternal rest and peace and tranquillity did nothing to assuage the awful gut-wrenching feeling of loss and helplessness at her passing

A year has passed and I still miss her terribly. Sometimes when I'm least expecting it, a wave of sadness and loss sweeps over me, and I just cry for no reason. Except, it's not for no reason. It's because that wonderful being, my mother, is gone from me. The grief that I have felt has made me realise that the bond between a mother and her child is so strong that it's as if the umbilical cord was never fully cut.

For all of these reasons, I am so glad that I had those seven weeks of leave-taking with her where I left my inhibitions and awkwardness behind and just opened my heart. It was a real gift, a privilege, and I know deep down that I made the most of it, because I already knew how awful it feels when that opportunity is not afforded us and it's quite simply too late. I was lucky. It wasn't too late second time around.

Our loved ones are just that – loved ones. Let's not risk feeling regrets when it's too late. If there are fences to be mended, mend them now. And talk the talk. Say the words. Once the words are uttered, they enhance the moment for the person who says them and the person who hears. And remember: that all-consuming love that we feel for our children, our parents have felt for us, their children, since the time of our birth. Today we follow in their footsteps, and the opportunities afforded to us in the now will never be afforded to us again, so seize the moment!

A True Visionary

Seán Weafer

IT HAPPENED WHILE I was having a pint in a Dublin pub, enjoying a colleague's company and conversation. We passed from the after work 'suited' drinks crowd to the time when the locals appeared to retake their rightful place at the bar and have their turn.

We were in mid-conversation when the form of the man silhouetted in the doorway took my eye. He was blind. I knew this because he carried a white stick and wore dark glasses. Pretty stereotypical, I'll grant you, but there he was nevertheless.

He seemed to be out of place among the remaining 'suits', who gradually started to inch away from him, myself included. If you'd asked us why, we'd probably have said we wanted to give him more room. But was that the reason? Or was it that it made us feel uncomfortable being around someone who reminded us that 'there but for the grace of God go I'?

The barman, who was dashing about serving the vociferous demands of the patrons, happened to glance up and see him edging forward. As the blind man carefully tapped his way towards the bar, the barman called out in a familiar tone, 'Hi, Jimmy . . . just go down the end of the bar there, and I'll serve you in a minute.'

Recognising the voice, the blind man smiled broadly and

shouted back, 'Jaysus,' he said in a strong Dublin accent, 'sure I could do dat wit me eyes closed!'

As the men surrounding us roared with laughter, I thanked the Creator for this little reminder that one's attitude determines one's quality of life and the mark that we leave on the fabric of history.

In the Face of Enemy Fire

Anne-Marie Coen

OLD ALEX GLANCED anxiously at the ominously darken-ing sky, then, pulling the door firmly to behind him, set out along the rough country road on the three-mile walk which would take him to town and the post office, for today was pension day. The December afternoon was bleak, and he shrugged his slight frame deeper into the black Crombie overcoat that he habitually wore, a relic of former, more affluent times, when he had lived in a beautiful house and his life had been very different. He sighed wistfully and fell to remembering.

He could still remember the elegant house in Belfast where he grew up as a boy with his brothers and sisters. He could recall the colourful garden and the swing that had hung from the oak tree there. He visited again, in memory, the well-stocked orchard and the stables where the horses lived, and smelled their horse smells and heard their excited whinnying whenever anyone approached. But most of all he remem-bered the 'factory', that vast vaulted workshop where his father had spent his time, plying his beloved trade, inherited from generation after generation of Langleys, of furniture making, wood carving and treen turned on the handed-down, handmade pole lathe, destined to become the last of its kind in the British Isles. Here Father would work all day long and often into the night, too, turning out the works of art necessary to fill the orders which poured in from all over the world for his much sought-after creations, many of which survive today in homes, churches and museums worldwide.

Alex could still smell the distinctive aroma of sap and wood shavings, oils and varnishes, which hung about the factory, aromatic, exotic, like the interior of some Eastern palace such as his sister Aoife was for ever inventing stories about. He remembered the apprentices, Jack and Benny, the former, strong and silent, and the latter, Benny Brice, bright and cheerful, bubbling with life, and how Martha, his eldest sister, had lost her heart to this gentle, lovable chap, and how she had cried when Father had forbidden their engagement and sent the love of her life away, out of his house, out of his business and out of her life, for ever. Mother had wanted them to run away together to her relatives in Scotland. They were in business there and would have looked after the young couple, seen them right. She'd offered them their fare and enough money to tide them over until they got on their feet. But, fearing her father's wrath, Martha had decided against such drastic action and had bidden her love goodbye for ever. She'd eventually married the beau whom her father had considered suitable – a man who adored her as much as Benny Brice had – but she had never known a moment untainted with sadness and regret from that day to this.

Alex shivered, as much from the still painful memory of the day they had packed up and left, for ever, the home of his childhood as from the effects of the bitter east wind which gusted maliciously about his sparse frame and tore at the old coat and scarf, almost taking his breath away with its strength. He could hear Father informing his children (none of whom had wished to succeed him in his line of business, the work being too hard, the hours too long and their taskmaster an unrelenting one) that the North had become a difficult place to live in. Sectarianism was rife, children of families with nationalistic tendencies were subjected, on their way to school, to name calling and stone throwing; their womenfolk, about their daily business, to sexual harassment; and the business premises of these same people were liable to attacks of vandalism. The reverse took place, too, but not at the hands of the Langleys, for whom the motto *live and let live* was sacrosanct.

So Father had decided to sell their beautiful home and his beloved place of work and return to the small southern town where he, himself, had grown up and had always had a hankering to return to someday. And they had gone there, to another house, beautiful too, but with a less fascinating workshop attached to it, and here Father had worked at his trade almost until the day he had died, when representatives of the National Museum of Ireland had come and asked if they might have his lathe and any pieces of his work available to put on display there; likewise the Keble Museum of Oxford. Alex had grown up here, a quiet, studious boy, gifted with an extraordinary memory for facts and figures. He had the works of Shakespeare by heart, could quote at will from the master, and was consulted by a famous company of Shakespearean actors whenever they visited the town, when they would spend all night discussing the merits and demerits of the bard with this extraordinary young man. Likewise, he was regularly consulted upon questions of history, science and current affairs, for it was generally acknowledged, that in matters of knowledge, Alex Langley was second to none.

But that was all a long time ago. Nowadays, he lived with his brother Jamie in a small, run-down soldier's cottage in the country, miles from the town and its conveniences, two elderly bachelors with their two dogs, several cats, a pet crow, Nedo the donkey and not much else to show for their lives. The rest of the family had gone long ago and made lives for themselves elsewhere. Two of the older Langley boys had remained behind in the city to continue with their studies, and two of the older girls had married there. Patrick had gone to America where he'd made a vast fortune only to lose it all again in the Wall Street crash. He had made it back on top eventually, for he was a strong man with a will of iron who refused to take anything lying down. He had married, too – a beautiful English woman, who had stood by him through thick and thin – and they had three beautiful children. Alex had never married. He had been in love though, oh, so much in love with Stella, the girl who helped his mother with the housework, a wonderful girl who had meant the world to him. But Father had interfered in his life, too, had forbidden their relationship, and fool that he was, weak, pathetic fool, he had bowed to his father's will and let her go. He'd never forgotten her, never stopped loving her in all the years since, when, having fallen in love with his happy-go-lucky charm, she had eloped with his younger brother, Frank to Australia, where they lived happily until the day she died at a tragically young age.

His brother and house-mate Jamie had never married either, probably because he'd had so many admiring young ladies to choose from that he had been unable to choose. Jamie had been a bit of a toff in his day, a favourite among the eligible women of the district and beyond, given to sporting pearl-grey suits and matching top hats on his trips to the races, his trademark, a gold handled walking cane which converted to a seat, accompanying him on all his outings. His consuming passion, though, had been for collecting antiques, and he had attended auctions religiously, filling the house with beautiful and valuable pieces of furniture, paintings and objects d'art, which he often, in turn, bestowed upon some individual who had taken his whimsical fancy and who had expressed admiration for some piece or other.

It made his brother's blood boil to think of it! Especially when there had been Margaret, widowed, with all those children to bring up alone! She could have done with some of the money which had been squandered on her brother's friends! Oh, well, there was no use dwelling on that. The children were all grown up now and gone their separate ways, all having done very well for themselves, for they had inherited the Langley looks and intellect. But they could have had an easier childhood; he shook his head sadly.

And Jamie was a hero, too, if an unsung one. He'd come home from the Great War decorated 'for bravery above and beyond the call of duty in the face of enemy fire'. He had risked his own life to save others from death. Upon one occasion, he had come running from the trenches amid a hail of enemy bullets to rescue an officer, a personal friend from his own home town, who had been wounded and lay incapacitated on the no man's land beyond. Jamie had thrown the man across his shoulder and run back with him to the relative safety of the trench, thereby saving the officer's life. But he'd come home to no bands playing, no flags waving, an unacknowledged hero of an ignored war just like his four brothers, three of whom had died terrible deaths on the field of battle, and his sister Margaret, who had given up her teaching job in Belfast to train as a nurse, in order to bring aid and succour to the wounded of that awful conflict. But his brothers had been conscripted. Unlike Jamie, they had not chosen to fight for the army of the enemy, as the British were regarded in the Ireland of those days. They had gone to work in their uncle's business in Scotland and had been forced to fight for a cause they did not espouse, and even considered traitorous to an Ireland in the throes of rebellion against the very country they had been coerced into swearing allegiance to.

One of them, Owen, sent to India, had been so incensed by the executions of the leaders of the 1916 Easter Rising in Dublin, especially the shooting of the wheelchair bound James Connolly, that he, and other Irish soldiers like him, had lain down their arms and refused to fight. They were subjected to brutal torture for their 'insubordination'. Many, including Owen, a young man, with a young family, died soon after the war had ended, from health problems caused by the inhuman punishments which had been inflicted on them, in his case having been tied to the wheel of a great gun under the burning Indian sun by day and the extreme cold at night. Alex could still remember when his brother had come home to Ireland, a shell of his former self, an emaciated, sallow man, huddled in an armchair by the fire, a heavy shawl around his thin shoulders. That was how he had remained for the six years leading to his premature death at the age of thirty-nine, which had left his wife a widow and his two small children orphaned. But they, in their turn, had left their home and realised their ambitions, Jane becoming a nurse and Henry a photographer with the *Irish Press*.

But Jamie had volunteered to fight in the Great War 'to strike a blow for democracy and the freedom of small nations'. His father, despite his obvious Anglo origins, was an Irishman to the core, a staunch patriot who had been so angered by his son's – as he perceived it – disloyalty, that he'd refused to purchase a commission for him, forcing him to endure the length of the war as an enlisted man, and all the disadvantages which went with it. But he had, eventually, accepted his son – his lungs badly damaged by the mustard gas with which the soldiers had been constantly bombarded – back into the fold. Alex had never forgiven him for his *lapse*, and to this day, the brothers still argued bitterly about the politics of that long ago era.

The old man had reached the outskirts of the town. His trek took him past the house where he'd spent his youth. Someone else lived there now, soaking up its comfort and elegance. He could see, through the window, as he passed by the low hedge, a huge fire dancing in the hearth, searing its way up the chimney, filling the air with the fragrance of turf fumes and the promise of warmth and cheer. He sighed deeply as, shivering, he pulled the overcoat tighter about his slight frame, and trudged on. Why had they ever left there and gone to live in that decrepit old place in the middle of nowhere? Jamie's doing, of course. He was entitled to the cottage and to the pension, paltry as it was, that went with it, he'd said. Hadn't he fought in the war and suffered greatly as a result? There had been no arguing with that. And with his inheritance sadly depleted, Alex had been in no position to keep up the big house alone and had no choice but to make the move with his brother. And so, they had come to this, a dreamer and an unsung hero, with a glorious past now only a memory, a miserable present and an uncertain future, and their hearts full of regret for what might have been.

The small post office was busy when Alex entered, full of people anxious to send off last minute Christmas cards and parcels. And, of course, there were the others, like himself, old folk there to collect the pitiful pittance which was their pension. Biddy Malone, the post mistress, sat behind the counter, her gimlet eyes peering over the horn-rimmed spectacles, hard and bright like the eyes of a bird of prey, her wizened face even more dour and peevish than usual, due to the increase in the mass of humanity pressing about her. She was infamous for her whole-hearted contempt for the human condition in general and the old and infirm in particular. Her rudeness when dealing with the public was legendary, and her incivility had earned her notoriety in parts even beyond the boundaries of the small community where she held sway. Children were often threatened with, 'If you don't behave yourself, Biddy Malone'll get you.' That was usually good for a quiet hour or two.

Today, she was outdoing herself. Having soundly ticked off a deaf elderly man for mishearing her directives, she flung the pension with such violence at an arthritic old lady that it had scudded across the counter, landing with a plop on the ground. The woman, too frightened to complain, had picked up her miserly allowance and scurried from the place, glad to have gotten off so lightly this time. The servant of the public now turned her malevolent attention upon the slight old man, fumbling ineffectually for his pension book through the many pockets of the worn, black coat and, after regarding him scornfully for a moment, suddenly barked, 'What what do you want?' Alex paused in his searching to study her sharp, embittered face for a moment.

'No wonder you were disappointed in love,' he thought dispassionately. 'The man who let you down had a lucky escape!'

He drew himself up to his full height, and with a degree of dignity that was awesome to behold, replied with old world stateliness to her viciously voiced question, 'A little civility for a start!' There was a stunned silence, as the customers stared from the frail pensioner, magnificent in his daring, to the scarlet face of the astonished post mistress, totally unused to having her autocracy challenged in any way. Suddenly, applause broke out in the tiny post office.

A Parent's Love

Gabriel Fitzmaurice

How close the sound of laughter and tears!
My children watching Dumbo on TV
In the next room–are those wails or cheers?
At this remove their screaming worries me.

Do my children laugh or cry in the next room?
I check them out and this is what I see–
No light illuminates the fading gloom,
Instead of watching Dumbo on TV,

High jinks on the sofa – they're both well,
I tick them off, their giggles fill and burst,
A parent's love knows all there is of hell–
I hear them play and strangely think the worst.

Maura's Story

Molly Harvey

IFIRST MET Maura in the school playground, waiting like all the other mums for the bell to ring, when all the children would rush to stand in line and wave goodbye as they started another day at school. I was back home on holidays taking my niece to school, and Maura was a newly acquired friend of the family; young children have an endearing knack of introducing parents to each other.

Maura was tall with sparkling eyes and always positive, even though she had obviously had a hard life. In April 1999, just a few days after our meeting, she was in Ardkeen Hospital where she was given the news that nobody wants to hear – the test results were back and her cancer was terminal. Her immediate thoughts were for her youngest daughter, Sinead, who was only two years old. On the morning the specialist broke the news to her, she turned to him and asked, 'How long do I have to live? Don't pull any punches; I've got things to do and plans to make.' The specialist told her that the normal life expectancy was between three and eighteen months. However, due to the cancer being so advanced, in her case it was more likely to be three months.

Maura left the hospital that day in a complete daze, drove from Waterford to Portlaw and knocked on our door. To begin with she was inconsolable with the thought that she wouldn't be there for her two girls. She would never get the chance to see Sinead make her Holy Communion, or to see Grainne bring her first boyfriend home. After a few strong cups of coffee and many tears, her mood changed and she was back to the positive woman I'd met in the school playground.

'Feck it,' she laughed, 'if I've only got three months, I'll make sure I'll have a great funeral planned.'

Maura called the priest from our house that day and arranged a meeting with him. Her funeral was going to be something else. She wanted a singer who would sing 'Isle of Hope' and 'The Foggy Dew', with balloons on each pew and a party afterwards. At first the priest felt very uncomfortable about the balloons and the singer. What would the parishioners think? However, Maura's strong will and attitude won him over.

When we speak from our hearts, it is as if we help other human beings dance and sing. Our warmth and passion flows from us to them. The true depth and rhythm can be felt and heard in our words. I know that I am most fully humanly alive only when I speak and live from my heart. It is as if we vibrate on a higher level. Maura proved that when we let our words be warm and positive we can watch magic unfold.

I kept in touch with Maura when I returned to England and on my increasingly frequent visits to Portlaw. We had many laughs together over the next year as she told me her plans for her funeral, and, to be honest, we forgot about her dying! She would always set herself small goals, and one of those was that she would live to see Sinead skip into school. That dream came true in September 2001. I couldn't miss that, and I was at the school that morning as Maura walked up the steps with Sinead.

The pride on Maura's face was there for everyone to see; the only thing that outshone it was the smile and the glow of happiness from Sinead, with her pale blue blouse and crisp navy pinafore and her shiny black shoes. I could see

Maura was getting weaker, but she was not yet ready to go. She asked me to take her into Waterford where she bought loads of birthday and Christmas cards. Then she went home and wrote them all up, putting a special message in each card up until the girls' eighteenth birthdays. I remember being choked with both emotion and admiration at her will to live.

Paddy, her husband, was weary by now and was finding it very hard to cope, especially when Maura asked him to take her and the two girls to Dungarvan, to a jewellery shop. She wanted each of them to pick out a piece of jewellery that would be put away for their eighteenth birthday. Paddy agreed to take Maura even though his heart was broken. A week later she was admitted to the hospice.

I rushed back to Portlaw again so that I could be with her, as we all thought that this was the end. Knowing Maura, I should have known better. She had other ideas, and I got a phone call from her on the Friday morning asking me to come and bring her home as she was signing herself out; she had a surprise booked for her husband. Off I went to collect her, really curious as to what she had planned for Paddy. I helped her to the car, knowing she was in pain, but she never complained.

I will never forget the look of surprise on Paddy's face when he opened the door that afternoon to see Maura and myself. Well, she had booked a weekend away in Salthill, County Galway, in the hotel where they had been on honeymoon fifteen years earlier. They had a great weekend together.

Maura passed away peacefully in March 2002. She had outlived everyone's hopes and expectations. She was a true friend who taught me many lessons in life.

Laugh a lot.

Don't take life too seriously

Live one day at a time instead of trying to reach tomorrow before it comes.

The Letter

Ultan Cowley

FOR ALMOST TWENTY years Sean Hynes, the postman, did his rounds by bicycle. From the post office he cycled thirty miles each day along both sides of a remote valley in the West of Ireland. In the little farming community, few households had occasion to receive post on a daily basis, and on most days he was finished in good time to get his own small herd of cattle fed and watered well before dark.

But Fridays were different. On Fridays almost every house along his route received a letter – always with a foreign post-mark, usually British but in some cases American – and in the lean decades following the war, each of those letters contained a cheque, or cash, or a postal order from a son or daughter. Their remittances were each family's financial life-line. This round took almost twice as long as usual, but neither wind nor weather could deter Sean or prevent him from delivering the precious post each Friday without fail.

In that denuded landscape, each house was visible from almost all the others, and the postman's route was monitored as the bicycle progressed along the valley's sides. The community could measure the devotion and diligence of an absent child by the regularity with which a household was seen to receive the Friday letter. The owners of those houses that escaped scrutiny on Fridays were watched to see whether a visit was paid on Saturday morning to the pub-cum-grocery or post office, where cheques, dollars, sterling notes or postal orders could be cashed and precious supplies purchased.

When a family showed signs of prospering on regular remittances, neighbours would say of the absent child, 'Isn't he/she the great rearing, surely?' Shame was cast on any home with absent sons or daughters which the postman passed by regularly on his Friday round. The culprit was usually male – perhaps a son working on the buildings in England where, it was assumed, he had become too fond of the drink.

Most parents had two or more children 'over', so it was difficult to tell for sure whether any had gone to the bad or were neglectful in their duty to those at home – and Sean could be neither tricked nor cajoled into giving such information away. But one household in the valley had no such protection.

Mrs Doherty was a widow. She had lost her husband just after the birth of their only child – a son – when a bull with an evil disposition crushed him against the wall of the holding pen, moments before being loaded up to go for slaughter. They had both married late in life, and the widow's age, along with the smallness of her holding, worked against her finding another man to take her husband's place.

Without a father to guide him into manhood, the son, Patrick, knew no boundaries and gave his mother endless grief. He hated farming. In the drive to rebuild Britain after the war, thousands of young men found well-paid work in construction. Most of his school friends did the same. When they came home to visit with their shiny suits, Brylcreemed hair and bulging wallets, he was envious and longed to follow them. As soon as he could persuade a friend home on holidays to lend him the fare, Patrick took the boat to England. He was used to hard work out of doors and quickly found work on a London building site. He was barely seventeen.

A month after his leaving home, a letter came from Patrick, for the widow, containing two £10 notes. Never a great scholar, his writing was a laboured scrawl of shaky capitals and extended to just a couple of sentences followed by a printed signature. But the vital money was the all-important thing, and the widow was comforted in the knowledge that her Patrick was a good son after all.

This became a pattern, and for almost a year, the widow mounted her bicycle on Saturday mornings once a month and went proudly into the village grocery to buy her bits and boast about how well her Patrick was getting on. But then the letters stopped. Inquiries addressed to Patrick's London address, a hostel in Charing Cross, were returned marked 'Gone away'.

People wondered if it was the drink had got to him. Or speculated whether perhaps a trench had collapsed on him, maybe while he was working on false cards or under an assumed name to avoid tax, so that no one knew his next of kin, or if he'd simply gone on tramp with one of the old Long Distance Men – the 'Pincher Kiddies' who had turned their backs on Ireland and lived in isolation by their own rules.

The widow, struggling on her small pension and relying on neighbours to save turf for her or get her cow in calf, aged visibly. She stopped going to the village unless absolutely necessary, other than for mass on Sundays. People worried that her health would fail or her spirit break.

Then, one Christmas Eve, the postman brought a letter. In it was £20 in sterling and a laboriously printed message on lined notepaper. It read simply, 'Happy Christmas, Mam. God bless, Patrick.' The widow was overjoyed. Patrick was alive, after all, and he hadn't forgotten her.

No more was heard from Patrick until the following Christmas, when another letter came with £20 and the same brief message. And so it continued, Christmas after

Christmas without fail, for fifteen years until the widow died. The postman knew well that, while the money was important, what sustained the widow through her long years of loneliness and isolation was the status that The Letter conferred on her in the eyes of her community.

It was only many years later, after he had retired, that Sean revealed to a trusted friend a secret which he had kept closely hidden until then. Patrick's Christmas letter, he told him, had been written by himself. Each year he'd had it posted from London by his sister, who had settled there when she was young, and delivered it himself. Yet sometimes, as the years passed and no other news of Patrick came back to the valley, he'd wonder if the widow's smile of gratitude wasn't a little warmer than the letter's meagre message seemed to call for. But he never inquired. 'Let the hare sit,' he'd say to himself, and cycle on . . .

Campaign and Count

Marian Harkin TD

O N A MONDAY afternoon in mid-March 1999, I put my head above the parapet and announced my intention to run as an independent candidate in the European elections the following June. About fifty people, family, well wishers, colleagues and friends, turned up showing their enthusiasm, support – and anxiety. I had no political experience, no idea how to run a campaign, no money and no party machine. Although I didn't appreciate it at the time, however, I had assets that were far more valuable – people who, over the next three months, would move heaven and earth to try and get me elected.

I had the optimism and the naivety to take on the system and the political parties, and for some reason I have never quite fathomed out, a sense of goodwill towards me began to emerge and grow as the campaign moved up a gear. In fact, it started that very evening when a woman from Claremorris, who described herself as 'a widow like your-self', rang me to say she was delighted I was running and that she would send a cheque for £100. I didn't know her and she didn't say it, but somehow I knew that £100 was a lot of money to her; she was placing her faith in me when she wrote that cheque.

My constituency of Connacht/Ulster was huge – but I wasn't starting quite from scratch. For a number of years I had been identified as one who made the case for the West of Ireland, so I was not an unknown at some of the doors I knocked on.

Our first hurdle was the posters. We ordered 5,000 cardboard posters and started to put them up, but within two days they were collapsing; a shower of rain, a gust of wind and Marian Harkin was disintegrating on the telegraph poles.

My campaign manager (a mother of three small children who took unpaid leave to do the job) decided that, to withstand the ravages of an Irish spring, each poster would have to be glued individually to pre-cut pieces of chipboard. Her shed became a poster factory. Her husband burned out the motor of his electric saw cutting thousands of pieces of chipboard. Volunteers were drafted, and reluctant teenagers were press ganged into hard labour gluing thousands of posters.

Two days after they were erected, the posters started to peel off the chipboard; the glue wasn't working! Back to the drawing board. A different glue was used, and on the third attempt the posters stayed up. The only time I felt jealous of other candidates was when, in the space of about three days, their beautiful cardboard posters were erected by a professional company all over the constituency. Yet, despite the fact that our homemade effort used up vast amounts of time and energy, and I relied on people to take their own cars and equip themselves with hammer, nails and tie backs, the mammoth task was completed. From Greencastle in County Donegal to south of Gort in Galway, from east of Castleblaney to the Atlantic at Belmullet, we covered the constituency.

People started to come on board, donations started to arrive, fundraisers were organised, a manifesto was drawn up, strategies were discussed, debated, decided and then, sometimes, disregarded. Press statements were issued, radio and TV interviews took place, leaflets were printed, car stickers were distributed, lists, and longer lists, were drawn up. The 'To Do' book became a nightmare. An election office was opened, phones started to ring, faxes to bleep, e-mails started to arrive, canvassing guidelines were drawn up, car-pools were organised, a hundred different things happening simultaneously. Like an avalanche it was gaining momentum, and we didn't know if it would bury us.

The goodwill of the people astounded me. Pat Cox, current president of the European Parliament, came to address my fundraiser. I had met him only once before that, yet he took twenty-four hours out of his own campaign to help another independent. Tom Fox, RIP, an independent TD in Roscommon, left his sick bed (although I didn't know it at the time) and came to Cavan to nominate me. An aunt came from Coventry and spent six weeks, seven days a week, on the road canvassing. People took time off work, used up their holidays, their weekends, their evenings and their nights on my campaign.

My two sons, aged eighteen and fourteen, canvassed for me, but on his first day my younger son found that adults were not really interested in taking leaflets from a fourteen-year old on the street. After a while he started saying, 'I'm canvassing for my mother,' and everyone stopped. I can remember a windy day and a warm welcome in Belmullet, meetings with farmers in south Galway, getting drenched outside the races in Roscommon, shaking at least a thousand hands outside Pairc Seán Mac Diarmada in Carrick-on-Shannon where Leitrim was playing Roscommon, and then travelling to Clones and finding the town in a sombre mood; Monaghan had just been beaten in the championship.

On a warm summer afternoon, we were canvassing in the Claddagh in Galway. RTÉ were following me, covering the campaign for *Prime Time*, and the presenter asked, 'Do you have an opinion on the Schengen agreement?'

I nearly died. I didn't know about the Schengen agreement. 'No,' I said.

'Do you know what the Schengen agreement is?'

'No.'

At this point he finished the interview. Off camera, half laughing, half incredulous, I said to him, 'I'll kill you, asking me something I don't know about. You and your Schengen agreement!' My supporters, who had gathered around, burst out laughing; but we didn't know the camera was still rolling, and one week later the entire episode was broadcast. It was good television; it showed I was human, sometimes getting it right, sometimes getting it wrong, but being honest and not bluffing.

I saw my mother, a quiet woman with absolutely no public experience, take to canvassing like a duck to water. Sisters and brothers – I am lucky enough to have seven – aunts, uncles, cousins, relatives from all over the country walked the roads and manned the phones. School friends from years earlier contacted me, and nuns who had taught me as a teenager in boarding school welcomed me with open arms. A friend from Wexford with a lifetime's experience in the PR business sat glued to a chair in my office for over four weeks. He read fourteen regional newspapers every week and sent press releases to all of them. With one ear tuned to the local radio and the other to national, he provided up-to-the-minute information, and like everybody else on the campaign, he tried to give me good advice.

I met total strangers who said, 'I know you, I've seen your posters.' I stayed in a beautiful old house on the shores of Lough Foyle with a woman who contacted me just a few days earlier and offered me hospitality. Approximately £25,000 in donations arrived in a three-month period.

People fed me, drove me, humoured me, picked up my clothes, photocopied for me, minded me, tried to shield me from the worst of it, and everybody, everywhere, all the time told me to smile, smile, smile.

One of the worst days occurred just one week before the election. A busload were on their way to Moylough to canvass at a major sheep-shearing competition. That morning an opinion poll on the election in Connacht/Ulster put the three front runners at well over 20 per cent each and myself and another independent at 9 per cent each. They were analysing the results of the poll on national radio, and everybody on the bus was listening. They spoke of the other candidates, including one of the independents at 9 per cent, but they never mentioned my name and suggested the result was a foregone conclusion. Everybody on the bus was crushed; to get 9 per cent was bad, but to be ignored was devastating.

One of the highlights of the campaign was the day before the election. About fifty of us, armed with stickers, hats, flyers and flags left the office and called to every business and shop in Sligo town, shaking hands and having the *craic* with everybody we met. People were happy, upbeat, and the surge of goodwill we encountered lifted us even higher. We were on a roll. That evening about fifty cars left Sligo town in a cavalcade through Sligo and Leitrim, to Ballintogher – my home town – knocking on doors of neighbours and friends, and on to other local villages, Dromahair, Drumkeerin and Manorhamilton, my home for eleven years. We headed for the border in Kiltyclogher, circled the statue of Seán Mac Diarmada, on to Rossinver, to Kinlough and back to Sligo via Grange and Cliffoney, flanked by Classiebawn Castle and Donegal Bay on one side and Ben Wisken and Ben Bulben on the other.

The day after the election, the votes from Sligo and Leitrim were sorted in the Gilhooley Hall. We, like all the other candidates, were allowed six observers. My six arrived at 9 a.m., my brother-in-law, and five women dressed in jeans and frocks, to find a line of pin-stripe suited men equipped with briefcases and mobile phones. My crew didn't have a mobile between them. At just after 10 a.m. my director of elections ran to a neighbouring house, rang me, woke me (honestly!), and said, 'Get in here, you're doing mighty.' An hour later I arrived, and as the day wore on it was clear I was doing well in some places, not so well in others, and I had no hard information on several counties.

The next day, the day of the count, was a beautiful, warm, fine day. Ninety-five per cent of my supporters, including myself, had never been to an election count before, so many of us were mesmerised and unsure of the procedures. Before I went into the count centre, two good friends came out to my car and said, 'Marian, it's not looking too good, prepare yourself for the worst.' Other candidates' votes were piling up in bundles of 1,000, mine were not.

. One of my sons was more interested in chatting up the daughter of one of the other candidates than keeping an eye on his mother's votes. Two of my brothers were in Australia, and they rang my mobile every hour, on the hour. I was *realistic pessimistic,* and wanted to speak to someone who was *realistic optimistic.*

By 8 p.m. I was in the restaurant next door, ordering food and coming to an acceptance of the fact that this would not be my day when my sister came chasing in and said, 'Marian, we think you have over 45,000 first preference votes, and they're announcing the result of the first count in ten minutes.'

I looked at her and said, 'Go back, make sure. This can't be right, and I need to know before I go in there.'

Five minutes later she was back, still smiling. 'Yes, we're sure.'

I couldn't believe it. I was in there with a chance. We left the food, uneaten, to await the result of the first count. The night wore on with eliminations and distributions of votes. By 3 a.m. it was down to the wire. A government minister had been eliminated, and the distribution of his votes on the next day would determine the third and final seat. It was between me and the other independent candidate.

No, I didn't win that third seat, and at my party that night I saw grown men cry, men I hadn't known three months earlier.

But I'm a sucker for a happy ending. I had to wait three long years for the next election. If I had known it at the time, I might have faltered; three years is a long time to remain a maths teacher and keep a political profile, but I wasn't without help.

On 18 May 2002, back in the Gilhooley Hall, my votes did pile high enough, and I was able to prove that if you have the belief and the determination, and if you don't give up, you can succeed in anything.

A Mass-Going Atheist

Martin Malone

I BELIEVE IN God in times of pain and mortal danger. At such times I pray hard. For example, *'Jesus!'* is the first word out of my mouth, spontaneously uttered as the hammer hits my thumb.

So, I go to mass on Sundays in Kildare Friary, or White Abbey as it's known to others. I like the friars. I think there's an earthiness about them, an ordinariness. They have my sympathy, too, because these days it sure ain't easy being a priest. I was conned into returning to mass-going. My ten-year old son wanted to be an altar boy and serve with his cousin. My wife attends another church – so, Dad, will you bring me?

Yeah. Okay. What do you say?

After thirteen years of being in the wilderness with the occasional lapse to attend a funeral, a wedding (a funeral of sorts) or a baptism, what did I notice when I began again to regularly scale the hallowed steps again?

Firstly – the stoup – I could see the holy water had algae (kidding). Secondly and seriously, what struck me was the wall ornaments at the back, the latecomers; I mean why bother attending mass if you're going to lurk like a shadow or stroll in when the service is half over? As a fella who hasn't bothered with mass for years, I'd forgotten about this slap of bad manners our priests have to contend with Sunday after Sunday. If there were £20 left at the altar for being in time for mass – ah, the last would be first, only to find the shadows had already been and gone.

Something else – this collection business: you meet someone on the way in with a basket and you get two more while you're sitting down. Come on! There's a miracle being performed in my pockets week in, week out.

I haven't been able to bring myself to slide into the confessional, partly because I am well able to justify my sins and partly because I don't think a person needs a conduit to speak with his maker.

I envy those people who believe. Their faith is a gift and must provide them with a great inner strength. I try to pray – I try to believe. I ask for Jesus to 'Be real'. If He is, then all else will fit into place. If He's not, well then we're all merely cosmic dust, eventually.

I've travelled the Holy Land – Bethlehem's the only place I got a buzz, and that was caused by a rubber bullet whizzing past my ear. Errah, no, the buzz was alive enough in Bethlehem – I felt that something definitely happened there. But *doubt,* I reckon, is an incurable disease.

I wasn't long back attending mass when I was asked to hand around the collection basket. I did it for a couple of weeks, but then – well, I found the notion of handing around this second basket a little off-putting. Windows for the boys' school! Give us a break. What happened to the money collected in the town for the construction of our swimming pool? Lying in a bank account for what reason? Cut the red tape and buy the bloody windows. Pleaseee.

Between people arriving late, whinging babies and collection baskets whizzing around – how is a soul supposed to pray and pay attention?

Another thing I've noticed at mass – there are actually very few volunteers: readers, collectors, Eucharist ministers; these are the sort of people who infuse a community with zeal and spirit. They do things without fuss and do them because they see that they need doing. I've great respect for these people.

I'd love to read at mass, but how do you react when you espy someone with a pious face and you know that this piety runs only as deep as her make-up? Brazen it out? Or the man who's thinking to himself, 'They'd let anyone read at the altar these days.' And he'd be right, wouldn't he? For you see I wouldn't believe in what I was reading.

But believe me – I want to believe.

Who knows? Maybe. Someday.

And the lady with the pious make-up can go to hell.

At the end of mass I wait some minutes for my son and the other altar servers to collect the mass pamphlets, et al. I noticed that some of those people who arrived late for mass had left in a terrible hurry during communion time, and the shadows had lessened in number on the walls.

I usually light a few votive candles – it's damn hard to ignite these new sort of tea-lights; I much prefer the skinnier type – in memory of relatives and friends who have gone on ahead. If you want to say I'm praying for them, fine. A minute or so later, the following sometimes happens: I get a crumb of a storyline.

Like last week for instance: *She senses a coolness from people – that they'd walk the other way sooner than greet her. They wouldn't do as much to a murderer . . .* Possibilities there. Anyway I've digressed – forgive me.

School. Religion. I remember nuns trying to beat the faith into me. It was so important to them for me to know the Our Father and the Hail Mary off by heart. They'd have been better off teaching me the meaning of the words, their weight. But I guess those nuns were unenlightened.

My son appears from the sacristy, genuflects (call that a genuflect!) and comes to me smiling. I hope for his sake, my sake, and everyone's sake that Jesus isn't a Santa Claus phenomenon.

A Mass-Going Atheist

I wish I wasn't the blind man at the cinema.
And that's my prayer.

Angels!

Ken Bruen

MY FAVOURITE LINE is by the German poet Rilke: 'Each Angel is terrible.'

I'm Irish so I know that already.

Abba are having one of their periodic blasts of re-fame. The *Gold* album is being played constantly. The song in my head is 'I Believe in Angels'.

May Kennedy was my sister-in-law. She had the face of a cherub. With an Irish complexion and that small smile hovering, she went to mass every day.

But a cherub who fell to earth and suffered the torments of the unappreciated.

Her voice was crystal pure, and when she sang, you were uplifted.

My daughter, Grace, has Down's syndrome and asked me if God ever married. She lit May up. 'Grace is an old soul,' May used to say.

May loved horses. From time to time I'd get a whisper and call her; she never asked, 'Will it win?'

No.

She was thrilled I passed it on to her. The anticipation was her joy. Most times the horse won and she'd be delighted. She would immediately put something in the poor box of the church.

During my years of suicidal depression, before I got help, she helped me.

It's two years since she choked on a piece of meat. By the time she reached hospital, her brain had been without oxygen for twenty minutes. For six months she was in a coma. The Kennedys went to her every day, combing and washing her hair, talking to her. Her brother, Mark, sat with her every night.

He said to me, 'You see that little smile, she's already experiencing the mysteries.'

I was raging at the mystery of why the worst things happen to the very best.

The day she died, I turned off the radio. At her mass, it was a bitter cold day, but as Sonny Molloy sang 'Ave Maria', a shard of light lit the stained glass window, and an angel for one held moment was spotlit.

Coincidence.

I read that Danny de Vito credits his success to his angel. I wonder who Arnold Schwarzenneger gives the credit to . . . the gym?

There was a time when I listened to Willy Nelson. An album he did with Merle and Waylon. I played it out. The classic track . . . 'Angel Flying Too Close to the Ground'.

I played that image in my head for a whole year, and I can't recall it now.

A friend gave me a copy of *Botticelli's Angel* by Harry Cauley, and my first thought was, 'May will love this.' Call it an Irish gesture, but I wrapped it in cellophane and left it on her grave.

It's a novel that makes you want to believe, gives you a sense of wonder you know can't last. More's the Galway pity.

My mother died in December . . . a glass angel stood by her bed, and she said, 'See how it shines.' I didn't.

I had to go to Dublin to sign a deal for two new books.

Back at the hotel, I was channel surfing and *City of Angels* was on . . .

On the soundtrack was Bono with 'God Will Send His Angels' . . . and as the end credits roll, Sarah McLachlann with 'Angel' . . . from the lyric comes . . . 'In this dark cold hotel room' . . .

Yeah.

My daughter has huge welcome on my return and says, 'Look at the painting I did at school.' It's a crayon angel and a name on top . . . I can't quite decipher it, and Grace says, 'Dad, you're so silly, it's May.'

That evening I reflect on celestial beings and think my head is not filled with angels, but for a glorious moment, my heart is suffused with them.

Dabble Day

John Sheahan

'We'll have good drying today,' you'd say,
Your weather-eye reading the clouds;
'A good day for the "dabble",'
–A baby-word you mothered for us.

Steaming sink of kettled water,
Rich with Rinso suds;
Expanding bubbles, greedy for air,
Blinking back to nothingness.

In this symphony of suds
You baptised the sweat stains
Of our daily labour,
- Legacy of Adam's fall.

Your strong foam-sleeved arms
Restoring shirt and sheet
To Sunday grace
In the forgiving water.

Humidity surrendering to scullery walls;
Condensation indulging in its own calligraphy,
As you rinsed and wrung
To clothesline readiness.

A mouthful of clothes pegs, your third hand,
As you wrestled with pneumatic ghosts–
Bulging and billowing shirt sleeve and trouser leg;
Invisible air-people, claiming squatter's rights.

Triumphant over the unseen,
You'd admire your line of gymnasts
Frolicking in the breeze.
'They'll be dry in no time,' you'd say,
Proud of your weather forecast;
Pleased with your 'dabble day'.

In the fullness of time,
You'd surrender to the twin-tub,
And 'dabble'. .. .
Would be washed from your vocabulary.

Infinity

Dr Pádraig Patridge

IT WAS LATE on a mild and sunny Saturday afternoon. Dublin in early April. Down in the Ten Jars pub in what was left of old Whitetavern Lane after its recent renewal into neat rows of city apartments, internet cafés, fashion boutiques and antique shops. Temple Bars and prime locations. Cow's Lane ecomarkets. You had to get your bearings all over again and right from the start. Joey's buddies were already ensconced in comfortable high stools in front of the bar pondering upon the state of the nation, current affairs, the joys of life and the price of a pint since the introduction of the euro.

Joey entered the premises through a high-arched Gothic front door. Strolling in around 4.30 p.m., he made his way round the corner of the beautifully carved, shining and dark mahogany bar, which offered fine vantages and pleasant Victorian views. Subtle side doors and secretive snugs at the back. Toilets down the stairs. Cellars below. Red-black floor tiles underfoot. Grand masses of mirrors on the sides, hand-crafted, gilt and gleaming on edge. Images cast lightly to boldly rebound.

'Jubilation! Send out a cry of joy to the universe and to its infallible creator. If only we had the time to experience, enjoy and make an effort to even faintly understand the beauty of it all. Nature has already been consigned by many these days to the confines of IMAX cinemas, FTSE indices, web browsers and Sunday afternoon excursions with the family in cars. Oh to have wings and fly like a bird or fins and swim like a fish!'

Joey was always fascinated by the concepts of finity and infinity – the boundless eternity of space and of time and the infinite smallness of atoms and matter. Satellite dishes, atomic microscopes, particle accelerators. Greater minds than his had truly racked their intuitive and analytical brains on these subjects for millennia, but at the end of their days they hadn't managed to come up with anything better in the line of either simple and/or explicit explanation.

He reckoned that it would never ever be possible for humankind to understand this complex matter. Clarification would always remain hidden beyond the realms of maths, physics, genetics, philosophy and psychic analysis. We ourselves are part of the equation. That's what many appear to have ignored and to have somehow forgotten. How could we ever begin to assay the forces that set us in train in the first instance or attempt to fully comprehend a creation, which remains way beyond our collective and limited grasps? The creature cannot delve into nor will it ever fathom either its origin or its creator. Irrespective of prophetic and apostolic revelation or of Hubble's telescopic insights and excursions into uncharted space.

'The energetic is way beyond its energy, which it may have deemed fit to release in ginormous big dollops and deliberate small dabs. Big bangs how are you?' quipped Dan the Man. 'These are secrets that may someday, if ever, be slightly disclosed to searching scientists and humble believers in nimble nutshells of potions in portions in pots and in pans.'

'But that's not the point of it all,' maintained the Mighty Green, scratching his ear and appearing pretty perturbed at the thought of it all. 'It's all very fine bothering ourselves about primordial issues, but when all is said and done we should really be using our limited knowledge to enlighten, enhance, empower and enable our brief stay on this milkiest and most wayward of bluish green planets. After all, every one of us is for ever and at all times at the centre of time and space whether in conscious or in sleeping states, no matter when or wherever or however we are. Maybe this is what the Bible meant when it stated that we were all created in the image of God, all temples of His Spirit, all crucifying Christ in eterna and being eternally damned and saved for our troubles. Linear directions entering the circular vortices of an apparently chaotic and convoluted cosmos. There's something now for you all to be thinking about while I order another drink!'

'Zones of transition – that's what it's all about – parallel, interpenetrant and interdependent universes. Omnipresence withheld although we are always and for ever at the outset and beginning of spatial and temporal infinities at all times and in all places. Time-space procedural contexts. Integral elements of archetypal flux. A continuum of shape changers, shifting appearances and ephemeral forms. We're all construed of invigorated stellar dust, the remnants of some super bloody nova. Matter constantly in motion, what with solar systems, red suns, white dwarves, black holes and gravitational pulls.'

'Pull the other one, would ya! It's not in the municipal rules you see. Where we end up and if we end up is purely a matter for future speculation and deliberative debate.'

'What's the matter?'

'Is anything the matter?'

'Nothing at all really.'

'So don't be going abroad now bothering yourself about things that neither concern nor affect yourself in the very first instance.'

'It's all best kept hidden and stashed away safely for a dark and rainy day in that cornered place of the secret and salty and cellular old sign.'

'Down the stairs and out to the left, I presume, and a fine spring day to some! With Alice peering through her looking glass. And what do you think she saw? Easter eggs and Easter bunnies? Good fertile folky lore hanging around yellow forsythia bushes and purple magnolias scattering red squirrels and grey-collared doves in the due mortal process of their bucolic rogue rage. Even though the majority of the populace haven't the foggiest as to where it all originated in the first instance. Hidden here, down on your hunkers, hidden there, find and seek, hidden away, search and destroy!'

'Anybody for a wee saltarello to loosen up the limbs? *Kyrie eleison*, for there was certainly no mention of this kind of carry-on in that most famous of Middle-Eastern mythological bestsellers. Neither in the paperback nor in the hardbound editions. Isn't it marvellous? Christianity's resurrection imbued with the symbols of Celtic life and the living spirits of goddesses of old. Enculturation reversed with salutary missions of another kind. And by no means impossible.'

'Like the wearing of the green and the drowning of the shamrock on St Patrick's Day and druids setting up their seven-year flames and healing hot fires on Uishneach's green hill in the very middle of Ireland. Didn't the people come from all over the place at the time to source the light for their hearths on Bealtaine's fine eve? None of those fig-leafed shenanigans for those boys and girls. No way! For Banba and Baal were still very much the earth and the sun, the green and the blue, tying their eternal knots around tall trunks of *bíle* and of oak, perpetually giving birth to the Dagda – their son, and the Father of All. Or so they believed.'

'Before you were born you were dead and after you died you were born, again, on your head! Floating through the black darkness for ever alone and in peace with yourself. All around – bodies, lives, spirits, souls, material and immaterial, forms and reflections of great unknown compassionate images, always at the centre of eternal time and of universal

space. Very real but transient still – growth, decline, trans-
formation.'

'Simple thoughts, oblivious truths, omniscience. But I
wouldn't advise you in hindsight to think about it too much
if your bespectacled substitute high babies teacher is asking
your little six-year-old self to proclaim upon the merits of a
song called 'Nelly the Elephant'. The chances are you will
end up outside the classroom door having to explain to the
head nun why you are out there in the first place. She will
not be amused! Complex is nature, human interaction, and
being. Lines are seldom straight, but mostly curved. We're
all spores on the winds of change and of human remove.
Hardly gone though soon forgotten and seldom mourned
but for a faithful few.'

'But at least we're here nonetheless – with Easter lillies in
our lapels and palms in our hands. Not tops. I dare say it's
up the Republic and the Boys of the Old Brigade for fear that
the most Britannic of majesties himself will rise up from the
dead to our dread once again. I'm only joking! Sure hadn't
we better not be worrying about these kinds of things any-
more? Aren't they all in the past now? Like ships passing in
the night. Let's look to the future instead and get a move on
to our homes.'

'My parting words of advice – live well for today and let
tomorrows look after themselves, for whatever the process-
es, we're always on stage!'

They laughed, loudly together, and shuffled out the
crowded bar door into an ascending side street, and Joey
smiled at a girl, just arrived, who asked, 'Sorry, is this place
reserved?'

The Healy Cross

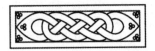

Yvonne Healy

I WAS THOROUGHLY enjoying, absolutely delighting in the tug-of-war over who would pay the bill. Delighting to look into my cousin's face with his huge Healy forehead and his fixed Healy gaze. I hadn't seen my cousin Richard since he was a baby, what with him living on one side of an ocean and me on the other. Finally, my father piped up, my father who was sitting there like a true old school Irishman staying carefully out of this particular monetary battle.

'Big-headed, pig-headed Irish, that's what you two are, as stubborn as your great grandfather, Con Healy.' I stopped, astounded. I'd grown up in a house where the word 'home' always referred to the country of Ireland and never the place where I lived. I'd grown up with all family in another country completely. Growing up without grandparents, it had never occurred to me that my father had a grandfather when I had not.

'Con Healy was a great man, an amazin' man altogether,' said my dad. 'He had the big Healy head, the outward sign of that family trait of resoluteness and steadfastness.' I thought to myself, 'You mean stubbornness,' and this coming from a man who once chased me ten swerving miles on curving country roads to give me a piece of mail that I, speeding away at seventy miles an hour and equally as stubborn, refused to accept.

Con Healy lived on a farm, which in 1880s Ireland was mostly fields; the trees long gone for English manor houses and nothing but bare hills left behind. A large farm it was. Con's father pig-headedly had gathered land going begging after the Great Hunger of 1849, two years of potato famine in which Ireland lost nearly a third of her population to starvation and emigration in coffin ships. Whole families lay in ditches on the side of the road, their homes burned behind them for non-payment of rent. Little ones starved in their mothers' arms watching wagonloads of food roll past their eyes. Food escorted by English soldiers to English ships, food grown by their daddies on tenant farms. Crops planted and nourished but never owned.

Hating the waste of good land, Con's dad had gathered it together and worked it with his son. But now Con worked it alone. Con was land rich but dirt poor. No man to help him did he possess – only strong shoulders and a steadfast heart. Shoulders strong from lifting hundred-pound sacks of feed and bran, seed and harvest. Strengthened this very day by lifting bag after bag, loading his donkey cart in trip after trip along the road between farm and mill.

At last, the cart was filled for the last time, Con led his animal toward home. He unloaded the cart and cleaned himself with a whistle on his lips. Time it was to enjoy the pleasures of the village of Macroom.

Having no alternate means of transport, no minivan or pickup, Con brushed his donkey clean and set out again along the lane from his house. Eastward on that road he travelled for the umpteenth time that day, and when the crossroads were reached, the donkey again turned to the mill on the right. Con pulled the donkey's reins to the left – to Macroom.

Now that donkey was no fool. Many the times it travelled the road that very day always turning to the right. And to the right again the donkey turned its head. The reins proving useless, Con slid off the donkey's back, planted his feet firmly and pulled the harness towards Macroom.

The donkey, as the beast is wont to do, refused to acknowledge human supremacy and sat itself down, right in the middle of the crossroads, refusing to budge one way or t'other.

But Con Healy had a plan to be followed, and the ever-resolute Healy walked himself round to the back of the creature. He positioned the massive shoulders and the large Healy head on the end where they could do the most good. Then Con pushed and heaved and shoved until that donkey finally faced left. Returning to the creature's nose, he picked up the reins expecting final obedience. But the donkey was having none of it. Its nose might be pointed one way but its feet were not moving at all, at all. The beast knew the right way to go, and no fool man was going to change its mind.

Con Healy bent his head until stubborn eye reflected stubborn eye. 'So that's the way of it, is it?' He took a deep breath, lowered his huge head forward and between the front legs, lifted the stubborn animal high on to his shoulders and began his slow, resolute walk towards Macroom.

'Now, it happened that some villagers were standing by the crossroads watching this drama unfold,' said my dad, 'and as the tale spread, that place in the road where those two roads meet became known as the Con Healy Cross.'

'It's true,' said my cousin as he swept up the bill and made his way to the cash register to pay, showing that very same family character. I looked over at my dad's big Healy head and for once noticed how well it fitted his shoulders, shoulders that looked bigger now.

Big-headed, pig-headed Niall Healy had carved a life for his family in a land both foreign and strange. His shoulders flexed strong from carrying his little ones to a better life for which they never thanked him. And I thought perhaps Con Healy's cross was an ass, but Niall Healy's cross was me.

Nicked

Gay Byrne

IWAS IN high babies in Rialto National School, on the South Circular Road. We lived a short walk away in Rialto Street, and on the corner of the street was Monaghan's grocery shop. On the way home from school one day, I took an apple from the colourful display of fruit and veg outside the shop.

Not being very bright, instead of eating the apple before I got home, I was still enjoying it when the Ma asked me where I'd got it. The only answer I could think of was that a man had given it to me. Wrong answer. Ma knew a lie when she heard one; she had a built in lie detector that would have been the envy of the KGB. She asked me again where I'd got the apple. This time I panicked and changed my story to a lucky find. The lie detector worked again, so she asked me a third time, and under this relentless pressure I cracked; I had no choice but to admit that I had nicked the apple from Mr Monaghan's display.

Solemnly and with a huge burden of sadness, Ma took down my savings box from its resting place. This was in the form of a little replica postbox, and you put the money in the slit that was used for posting the letters on the real one; there was no other opening in the box.

With the savings box in one hand and taking me by the other, Ma walked me slowly up to Monaghan's shop. It seemed to be a longer walk than usual, and when we got there it was pretty full of neighbours. Ma interrupted proceedings by announcing to Mr Monaghan (Christy to his friends, including Ma, but not to me) that this young man, her son, regretfully, had stolen an apple from the outside display. She went on to say that she, and he, had come to make restitution of the full retail price of the apple, and then, as I stood in shame, she handed over my savings box.

The assembled multitude looked suitably outraged that such a thing had happened in our neighbourhood, and there was much clicking of teeth and sad shaking of heads. There was also a knocking of knees from the little boy, but I'm not sure if they heard that.

To get money from the box was a work of art; you had to insert a knife in the slot, upend the box, and deftly coax the coins out one by one. Mr Monaghan had a stern nose and tended to glare over his spectacles at people, so as he stood looking at the box I wondered if he'd be able to get the money. No bother to him, he took out two pence, glared at me, handed the box back to Ma and made some comments about the appalling lack of morality in the world, and he wondered where it would all end.

Then he mentioned something about all of us being found dead in our beds. He paid tribute to Ma's integrity and honesty, and said how he hoped – nay, fervently prayed – that there would be no repetition of this heinous crime. He went on to point out that as long as there were a few people like himself and herself in the world then at least there was reason for hope, and blah, blah, blah . . .

I didn't pay too much attention to this – I had my little head down and the tears were rolling down my cheeks. Ma and I walked out of the shop, followed by the baleful stares of the entire street; it was a mixture of sadness and contempt for a miscreant caught in the act.

It was not further referred to in our house.

If Mr Justice Flood or Mr Justice Moriarty have an inclination to examine this matter, then I can tell them now that Ma is dead. So is Christy Monaghan and his missus, and all the neighbours in Rialto Street. There were no receipts.

I never nicked anything from anyone, ever again. God rest you, Ma – and Christy.

I Believe in Santa Claus

John Madden

IT WAS CHRISTMAS Day and I was just ten years old, an orphan in St Joseph's Boys School in Tipperary. The school was run by the Church as a home for orphans, and other children from homes where their parents were, for various reasons, unable to take care of them. As far as I can remember, there were about two hundred of us living there.

There was very little for any of us to look forward to throughout the year but, unquestionably, our biggest event was Christmas Day. That was the magical day when all of us young lads got to see our hero, Santa Claus, the only person who ever brought us presents.

Santa would arrive at the orphanage by coming up the long avenue, shaded by big trees that formed an arc high above the road. This avenue separated the orphanage from the main road, which went into the town of Clonmel, a place we dreamed of going to some day.

Santa Claus drove a team of four horses – although we all believed they were reindeer. The horses had a couple of bells attached to their halters, so we could hear them in the distance as they approached. And we, the children, would be standing outside in the cold at the top of the avenue, excitedly waiting, and listening for the sounds of the sleigh bells.

On the Christmas Day in question, we were waiting for an unusually long time. It was foggy and cold. As all of us children peered anxiously down the avenue, our teeth chattered and as time dragged on, our faces saddened; there was no sign of Santa and we could hear no bells, except in our over-active imaginations.

Rumours went around like wildfire: 'There's going to be no Santa this year . . . Sure, didn't he get lost or killed in the fog, there'll be no presents this year.' And I was desperately hoping for a cowboy outfit. Some of us started to cry. How could this happen? How could he not be here? How could he let us down?

Our minders had started to usher us back inside the building when my best friend, Paddy O'Leary, shouted, 'Wait, listen, I can hear the bells!' We all spun around and ran back out. As we gazed down the avenue, straining to see through the fog, we saw a light, and we hoped against hope that it was Santa's lantern. We ran forward, ignoring our minders' efforts to keep us in an orderly line.

The light got bigger as my eyes widened, and I could feel tears of joy rolling down my cheeks as the sound of the bells got closer and closer. And then, emerging from the fog, we saw the heads of the horses with steam bellowing from their nostrils. It was the best moment of my life.

Santa had not let us down: he and his horses were the most beautiful sight I had ever seen. I got the cowboy outfit that I'd asked for, and Paddy O' Leary got a big game of Snakes and Ladders, which we played three times that day.

And once again, I believed in Santa Claus.

Changing Direction

Gerard Hartmann

IN AUGUST 1991 I thought I was the fittest man in Ireland. I had just won my seventh national triathlon title. It was a tremendous feeling; I felt like I was floating on air with the world at my feet. Four days later I was out on my bike, back in training in Florida, and in one split second my competitive career ended. It was a clear day, not much traffic on the road, and I was travelling at around thirty-two miles an hour when an animal – I'm not sure what – hit my front wheel. I went over the bars, the bike went one way while I went the other with the net result that I shattered my hip and had to undergo emergency reconstructive surgery.

As I lay in a hospital bed virtually unable to move for nine days, and then hobbled around on crutches for fourteen weeks, it seemed as if my whole world had come to a standstill. All my plans, all my goals, had been directed towards my sport, and now that was finished. I suppose I could have felt sorry for myself and looked around for sympathy from others, but instead I made a concrete decision: 'I'm down, but not out.'

During that period, when I was at my lowest ebb, I made the decision that I would take all the energy and enthusiasm I had as an athlete and channel it into becoming the best physical therapist in the world. Note the words – not just *a* physical therapist, the *best* physical therapist.

That first year after my accident was the toughest period of my life. In one tragic moment on that road in Florida, my identity as a person and a world-class athlete had been taken away from me. My first challenge was to re-establish my identity and get myself accustomed to getting out of bed every morning with a new focus, a new goal. It was not easy, physically or mentally, but nothing worthwhile is ever easy, and all through this difficult time I had an inner belief that it was all part of God's plan.

Did I achieve my goal to be the best? That is a question for someone else to answer, but just one year later I was treating twelve Olympic medal winners at the 1992 Barcelona Olympic Games. Once again I felt like I was floating on air. I had changed my focus, but I was world class again, and I have never looked back. Even through adversity, being positive, having faith and trusting in God is the only way I know.

As a result of my constant contact with many of the world's leading athletes, I am often asked what the qualities are that make successful sportspeople. My answer is simple – they are exactly the same qualities that make people successful in any other walk of life: desire, passion, perseverance and a genuine enthusiasm for whatever it is they do.

Ballymote Champion

John Perry TD

As THE BARQUE *Dromahair* sailed out of Sligo Bay in the autumn of 1848, Michael Corcoran stood on the deck and watched in sorrow as his homeland faded into the distance, believing he would never see it again. His premonition was right, and although he never did see Sligo or Ballymote again, his return was inevitable, and Ballymote did see him, 155 years later, in the form of a large bronze statue.

Michael's life was a classic hero's quest, but like countless others, that of a man not a myth. When his father died, eighteen-year-old Michael became the breadwinner and joined the Revenue Police, finding and destroying the *poitín*. It was a dangerous occupation, and they were more despised than the constabulary.

The winter of 1846-1847 was fiercely cold and snowy. Disease and starvation escalated, and suffering increased as paupers were evicted and families broken by unemployment, death and emigration. Those were hellish burdens for young men who saw more illness, misery and death than they ever imagined, without having any realistic hope to offer. Private Corcoran became a Ribbonman, undertaking midnight missions that were meant as deterrents to those who evicted, cheated or harmed helpless people in any way. Michael kept up his dangerous double life for almost two years and then, for reasons unknown, resigned abruptly and booked passage to New York.

He disembarked in New York City with a queasy stomach and empty pockets, but it was here, in America, that Michael was to make his name. Starting out as a clerk in a tavern, he took over as manager when the proprietor died. He became an American citizen, was drafted into the state militia as a private in the 69th Regiment, and in the space of three years was promoted through the ranks to captain. A senior officer described him as '. . . the best, if not the very best, infantry officer in the 4th Brigade'.

He was seen as a rising star in Democratic politics and someone who could deliver the Irish vote. In 1859 he was the first American to join the Fenian Brotherhood and was soon their military commander. In the militia he was promoted to colonel of the 69th Regiment. Then it all fell apart. In late 1860, the nineteen-year-old Prince of Wales visited New York City, where there would be huge celebrations, including a ball to which Colonel and Mrs Corcoran were invited. Michael wrote a polite note declining and refused to order his men to parade in honour of the prince. They had lived through a famine during which more than a million Irish people emigrated and even more had died as a result, many believed, of Britain's tepid concern.

Many New Yorkers were outraged that this ingrate Irish immigrant had the effrontery to insult the royal guest of the city, demanding that his citizenship be revoked and that he be thrown out of the country. A court-martial was ordered at the same time that Abraham Lincoln was elected president and the southern states began seceding from the Union. The Irish community in San Francisco sent Corcoran a one-pound gold medal, and the one in Charleston sent an ornate gold-tipped palmetto cane, both in admiration of his integrity and for backing his men.

When the Civil War began in April 1861, Lincoln called

for volunteer militia units to defend Washington DC, and the 69th Regiment voted to answer the president's call. Colonel Corcoran's court-martial was dropped, and the 69th prepared to go to war. In an about-face, flag-waving New Yorkers cheered them as they marched to the docks with the colonel riding in a carriage, too weak to walk or ride a horse following a debilitating illness. In Washington DC they were joined by Captain Thomas Francis Meagher's Irish Zouaves.

The militia units were within days of returning home when combat exploded near a creek called Bull Run. The Confederates won the battle, and Michael Corcoran was wounded, captured and imprisoned. He was repeatedly offered parole if he would vow not to take up arms again, but he always refused to leave his men. A Confederate officer informed Corcoran that he was now a hostage and would be the first officer hanged in retaliation if the Union hanged some southern privateers the Yankees regarded as pirates.

The Union attempted to have him freed in a prisoner exchange, but the South refused, believing that he was as much a hero to the Irish soldiers in the Confederate army as he was to those in the Union army. They feared that if Corcoran were released, those soldiers would desert and follow him north. After thirteen months they relented and he was exchanged for a Southern colonel, emerging from prison emaciated and weak.

Great celebrations greeted the exchanged prisoners, and Corcoran dined with President Lincoln who made him a Brigadier General. When Michael returned to New York to recruit Corcoran's Irish Legion, the largest crowd ever seen in the city jostled to see and salute him as he paraded up Broadway in a carriage. Everyone, even his former critics, hailed General Corcoran as a hero, a true American patriot. He accepted their tributes in the name of his soldiers, not his own.

Three different political parties asked Michael to run for Congress. He declined, not only because he had an obligation to fulfil, but also because he saw that William 'Boss' Tweed was trying to manipulate the election. April 1863 found General Corcoran commanding a division in Suffolk, Virginia. Late one night he was informed that their garrison was about to be attacked and that he was needed at the front. He rode off with an escort party, but a short way into the ride a man stepped into the road causing them to stop. The man, who sounded drunk, demanded the password. Michael gave his name and rank, but the man refused to give his and insisted that he would not let them pass. In a great hurry, the party started forward, and the general told the man that he must step aside. The man waved a sword, poked it at Corcoran's horse, then reached for his belt as to draw a pistol and shouted, 'Not for you or any other Irish son of a bitch!' Michael reached his pistol first and shot the man, who stumbled back and fell, shouting more curses.

General Corcoran told an aide to look after him and later learned that the drunken man, a lieutenant colonel, was dead. Michael requested a court of inquiry where he was judged liable for the officer's death, and a court-martial was ordered.

Shortly afterwards he received a telegram saying his wife had died suddenly. Michael went back to New York for the funeral, and then returned to Washington where he called on President Lincoln and asked to be transferred to a combat zone. He also learned that the court-martial had not been preferred yet because none of the commanders would chair it.

Then one day in camp, he fainted. The doctor said he was debilitated due to the prolonged imprisonment, malnutrition and exertion. He was told to rest, eat oatmeal and drink barley water. Frail and exhausted, Michael got married instead. His bride was the beautiful seventeen-year-old granddaughter of the man who had given him his first job in

America. Many believe this was an expression of gratitude; he knew he was seriously ill and that his substantial brigadier general's pension would help the family. He returned with her to Virginia as the new division commander in that theatre.

Although Thomas Francis Meagher had resigned his commission, he still spent time visiting some of the camps. Michael invited him and Mrs Meagher to stay with the legion at Christmas. Meagher spent a few days with him first and then went to Washington to escort his wife, and Corcoran's mother-in law, back to camp.

On the day the ladies were to arrive, Michael woke up feeling unwell but went to 6 a.m. mass as usual, had his coffee and then accompanied Meagher to the railroad station. As he rode back to camp slightly ahead of his escort party, his men saw him suddenly raise his hand as he rode around a curve in the road, out of their sight. When they caught up with him he was lying in a ditch having a violent convulsion. It was about two o'clock in the afternoon. The doctors thought a blood vessel had burst in the brain, causing his fall from the horse, and there was little they could do. Michael never regained consciousness and died at 8 p.m. that evening, 22 December 1863, aged thirty-six.

His embalmed body arrived in New York on Christmas Day. He lay in state in the Governor's Room in City Hall (where President Lincoln would lie just sixteen months later). The flags in the city flew at half-mast, and after the requiem mass at St Patrick's Cathedral, he was interred in Calvary Cemetery on Long Island, with his mother and first wife.

Meagher eulogised Corcoran a year later, saying that when the time came, Michael had 'wished and prayed and hoped to be laid to rest deep in the green sod, with all these familiar voices, with all these wild, tender, and glorious sights and influences about him'.

Welcome home, sir.

The Beggar

Martin Malone

WE HAD A bit of time to kill – we didn't know how much. Charlie Swing Gate was closed because of a shell warning and with it the road to camp. So, we headed to Tyre, that Biblical city mentioned so often in the Old Testament, from where Hiram sent the materials to assist Solomon in building Jerusalem's temple. Labourers for hire haunt the roundabout. Listless men drawing on Lucky Strike cigarettes, eyes carrying the squint of depression, time to rent but no one hiring, the morning pushing on.

A honking seaside road, full of smog, sun-hot metal, purring engines, leads to the port of Tyre. Swell of the city on Friday market days, stink of goat, and vegetable stalls. In the souk flies dance in crazy rhythms about a cow's carcass that hangs from a rusty hook.

We wear jungle greens and scuffed and scraped desert boots. Blue berets tucked under shirt lapels. Black brassard with MP in white on the right shoulder. Pens, like our pistols, holstered, our notebooks bulging in our shirt pockets, swollen with names of sinners we'd taken on the morning's speed check on the road to Sidon.

Peter had done something strange on the way to the souk. He said something I hadn't caught because of Arabic music blaring from a stall. Cupping my arm he said again, 'Do you see that woman?'

'With the baby, begging?'

'Yes.'

'Yeah, I see her.'

'She's a bluffer, a chancer – I was here six years ago, and she conned me out of $10. I heard afterwards about her and her fake sick baby.' I ask if he is sure, and he says he is. At the time he had thought she looked remarkably like his Aunt Doreen, and still she's the spit of her.

She doesn't recognise Peter because when she spots us she ambles right over, a slight woman in loose rags with a black headdress revealing only her olive-green eyes. Extending her hand, she keeps bobbing the baby up and down, saying 'medicine' over and over. It sounds like a chant.

I walk on, ignoring her, and Peter too. But then the most curious thing happens: he hurries back and thrust a bill into her hand and comes away from her shaking his head.

He's shaking his head at the mystery of himself.

Sitting to a table, its top covered with a candy-striped tablecloth and wooden condiments that closely resemble over-sized chess pieces, we order Turkish coffees. We watch an old man bake pitta bread, the aroma filling the room. I tell Peter that I'll pay for these – seeing that he had allowed himself to be fleeced.

Again.

'Why did. . .?' I begin to ask.

He shrugs, 'I don't know.'

'Not like you, not like a Kerry man to be caught twice,' I say.

'She didn't catch me twice – when I walked by her I saw the baby and I saw her – I gave her a hard look – then you know, I just got to thinking that she hasn't moved on in six years, so . . .'

'How much?'

'Twenty bucks.'

I want to make a crack about inflation but don't.

The Singer

Carmen Cullen

SHEILA WAS FIVE when her mother died. She was the second eldest of a family that included twins. This was a terrible tragedy, and the small town in County Tipperary where she lived rallied round with messages of help and support.

In the middle of all this the pain of the little girl was forgotten about.

'Don't bother your daddy with questions,' she was told by her aunt, her father's sister, who had come to live with them. 'He might get too upset.'

Then her father married again. The children need a mother, he was advised, and it was true he was lonely.

The family moved to live on a farm. It was an idyllic place to grow up, but once more the little girl was forgotten about. Sheila loved reading and books and withdrew into a make-believe world. She never presumed to ask for love and never got it.

It was only when her stepmother died and she moved up to Dublin and had children of her own that love blossomed again in her life.

She made mistakes. The past seemed to be always catching up with her. Then somebody gave her a photograph of her mother. She put it on her mantelpiece. She began to talk to the photograph. She asked her mother for help. She realised she had a right to a place in the sun, to show everyone who she really was. Her mother had been a singer.

Sheila began to work on her own voice, quietly at first and then performing a little. Soon she began to draw crowds. She is now a professional singer, and her songs can be heard on CD. 'My mother was a singer,' she would explain when asked about her talent.

At long last she had completed the circle, linking up, through the singing talent she had inherited, with a mother who died when she was five.

The Christmas Call

Michael Coady

OLD MOSSIE WAS one of those people who had somehow slipped into my life without my fully realising it. He lived down a narrow boreen, you see, on the way to a mountain lake in which I used to fish. He had got used to me passing the door of his little thatched house, and it seemed natural and normal to stop and chat so that gradually we got to know each other. He himself knew both mountain and lake intimately. Hadn't he fished that lake before I was born? And hadn't he seen that mountain at all seasons and in all weathers?

On my way back from an evening's fishing, he began to ask me in for a cup of tea by the fire before I'd walk out to where I had left the car near the main road. In the end this became a regular routine, and if the fishing had been good I'd leave him a fresh trout 'for the pan'. His wife had died years before, and if he had any children or relations then they were never mentioned. Someone told me that there was a son who had disappeared in England long years before. The truth is Mossie was hungry for a chat and some human contact. When the fishing season came to an end in September, it was like closing a door or cutting off a bridge.

'I suppose I won't see you again until the spring,' he'd say with a sigh.

'Ah, sure, I'll drop up sometime before then,' I would say,

and actually mean to do so, since I only live ten miles away down in the valley. Invariably though other things would intervene, and long months would elapse to the opening of another fishing season before I would stand again at the old man's door, trying to cover my sense of guilt with some joking remark about how he had wintered well.

And the time of year when I'd be least likely to be thinking of the lake, the mountain and the old man was on Christmas Eve, what with the shopping and hurly-burly of the town, the friends encountered on the streets and all the customary hustle and bustle of the season.

Well, one Christmas Eve came on which I had some kind of visitation. That's the only way I can describe it: some kind of call. I remember standing with the children listening to the band playing carols on the street when suddenly it was as if someone had invisibly tapped me on the shoulder or tugged at my elbow.

And in some uncanny way I knew immediately what it was. 'I'll make a run up in the car to check out if old Mossie Ryan is all right,' I said to my wife. 'I should have thought of it earlier. I'll be back in an hour.'

I quickly gathered together a little gift-box of food, with some tobacco (the kind of old-fashioned plug he liked) and a baby bottle of whiskey, and then I headed off along the mountain road, a route I hardly ever travelled in winter.

When I got to the thatched cabin through the mire of the boreen, I thought first that there was no one at home and was about to turn away. Then I heard a faint groan and I pushed the front door in. The hearth was cold; Mossie was lying in semi-darkness in his bed, grey in the face and was almost unable to speak. He pointed to his chest, and I knew he meant his bronchitis. 'It was God and His Blessed Mother that sent you,' he gasped.

I lit the fire and made him a hurried cup of tea. 'I'll be back shortly.' I said and rushed down to the crossroads to call the doctor. By nightfall Mossie was being cared for in the warmth and comfort of our little cottage hospital. We visited him there on Christmas morning. He was shaved and smiling, sitting up in bed and snug as a bug in a rug. 'I wouldn't have lasted out the night only for you,' he said. ''Twas the luck of God you came!'

Luck? That Christmas Eve taught me a parable in which I myself was made an agent. I had been made the instrument of providence in some simple but mysterious way that took me by surprise. And I learned also that Christmas can be a time of tightly shut family doors, which may unthinkingly exclude the lonely and marginalised who have most need of room within.

But Dreams Will Not Die

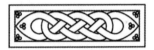

Miriam Gallagher

O N TRAMORE STRAND, during the summer of 1947, Margaret puts dabs of Nivea Creme on our upturned faces. She is brown as a berry. Her legs look as if she's wearing tan coloured stockings. She says we are lucky spending every afternoon on the strand, unlike other children, who only come here on their holidays. I feel there must be more to life than endless sand castles and trudging across acres of sand for buckets of seawater.

But this afternoon is different. It all starts with the sound of music, floating down from the prom above. Intrigued, I slip away from Margaret's watchful gaze. There will be hell to pay, but I am prepared to risk it for the chance of a lifetime.

On the prom a band of gypsies in brightly coloured clothes; men laugh and drink from brown bottles; an accordion player, with a cigarette dangling from his lip, begins to play a lively tune. A man, smiling with half-closed eyes, seizes a large gypsy woman around the waist. She pats her hair, fixes a neckline that barely covers her ample bosom. As they dance, her gold hoop earrings jingle. Gaily-coloured skirts whirl.

The man flicks his oily black hair out of his eyes, stamps with his boots. Twirling and panting, they sway first this way, then that. I notice beads of sweat on the man's face, on the woman's heaving chest. They are dancing with a wild abandon I have not seen before – even at the pictures. They end with a flourish, bow to the crowd gathering on the prom.

The gypsy woman catches my eye. 'Hello, little girl.' She beckons with a smile. 'Come and join the gypsies.'

She glances at the man, who throws back his head, laughing. He has two gold fillings in his teeth.

'Can I dance?' I ask the gypsy woman.

'Sure. But first will you hand round the cap?'

She winks in the direction of the gypsy boy, who is collecting money. I wrinkle up my nose when he presents me with his greasy cap. The gypsy woman winks again, this time at me.

Summing up the situation, I take my bucket down on the strand and approach a knot of people sunbathing beneath the prom.

'Help the gypsy dancers!'

Soon my bucket is half full of coins. At this rate the gypsies will want me to join them without delay. Excited at the prospect, I suddenly feel a hand on my shoulder. 'And what do you think you're doing?' a voice hisses. Startled, I turn to find myself facing Margaret. 'Wait till your mother hears about this!' Quick as a flash, the gypsy boy upturns the contents of my bucket into his cap and speeds off towards the prom.

Cheated out of my chance to join the gypsies, I am led away by Margaret. As I keep looking back over my shoulder, the gypsies on the prom get smaller and smaller until, like my dream, they disappear.

But dreams will not die. Many years later, as a playwright and screenwriter, I found myself writing a screenplay about my meeting with the gypsies. I framed the story around a present-day grown woman who remembers a childhood moment when magical gypsy music lured her away to a dramatic world of adventure and romance. I decided to make the film myself and took a course in film-making. Where better to shoot *Gypsies* than on Tramore strand? I was blessed with lighting cameraman Shane O'Neill, whose enthusiasm for the project equalled my own. As a first time producer and director, I was understandably nervous, but with skilful actors and a talented crew, all the hard work paid off.

The sun shone, the sea dazzled. My gypsy actors danced daringly, watched by an entranced six-year-old Roisin Deady, playing her first film role. Her actress mother, Audrey Behan, as the Gypsy Woman, flounced her petticoats as she swirled provocatively to haunting music, specially composed by Seán Molloy. In the final shot the grown woman, who was that little girl in 1947, smiles at her dream as she walks slowly out towards the gleaming Atlantic. Calling 'Cut' on that closing shot gave me a great sense of fulfilment.

After the fun of shooting came the hard work of editing and post production. At film festivals *Gypsies* provoked a warm response, and RTÉ wanted to broadcast it twice! By the summer of 1994, I had turned my dream into a film and brought it to the screens of Ireland, the UK, New York and San Francisco. During the Irish Film Festival, the festival's director, Grania Flanagan, told me, 'Miriam, I was just like that little girl. We all were.'

For me, whenever I watch *Gypsies* in cinemas, on TV or video, time melts away, and I'm back to the summer of 1947 when I nearly ran off with the gypsies.

The Other Big Fellow

Dr Liam Twomey TD

IN OCTOBER 1987 when I started studying medicine in Trinity College Dublin, one student stood out from all the others, not because he was 6ft 3in high and had the build of a circus strongman, but he was older than the rest of us. There were one or two other mature students, but this guy had a great personality that made him different.

Students are a very sociable bunch, and this man and myself became part of a group of medical students where we were learning to enjoy ourselves a lot faster than we were learning medicine. I was living with my brother at the time, but through a series of circumstances, I ended up having to share a flat with this big fellow. The only criticism I have of him to this day is that he is probably the messiest person I ever lived with in my life.

He had qualified as a PE teacher but did not like it and went on to become the European sales representative for an English company before deciding that he wanted to be a doctor. One of his outstanding qualities was a lovely singing voice, and in rural areas, where the closing time of the local pub had more to do with the a mood of the barman then that of the local gardaí, once this man started to sing, we knew we were there for the night!

He decided to have his voice trained, and at the age of thirty he enrolled for singing lessons. As friends are inclined to do, we mocked him relentlessly in the beginning because we just could not imagine this big awkward man as a singer, or even among singers.

In November 1993, our group headed off to the RDS to hear the final result of all these music lessons, and lo and behold, our friend added another distinction to his life when he won the John McCormack Cup. This heralded the beginning of a new era in his life, which saw him become a teacher, a doctor, a champion horse rider, a supreme athlete, a fabulous singer, a good friend and, perhaps most importantly, someone who knew no limits.

As a participant in two Paralympics, he won eighteen gold medals. I left out the fact that he is a double amputee below the knee, because this so-called disability has not affected my friend getting more out of life than the rest of our class put together.

But there is also a good heart behind all the fame and glory he has achieved. Long before Ronan Tynan became world famous as one of the three Irish Tenors, he promised to sing at my wedding. It was one evening after too many pints of Guinness, and certainly many years before I met my wife Liz, that he made this offer.

A few months after I got engaged, he rang to remind me of his promise and to say he would definitely be singing at the wedding. To put things in perspective, Ronan had already released an outstanding successful CD and at the time was recording his second one. He was already singing in New York and Milan, but he meant what he said, and he was going to do it. I don't think I heard from him for weeks before, and I panicked the night before the wedding when he did not show up in the hotel room I had booked for him. The morning of our wedding, the only person I could get in touch with was his sister, and all she could tell me was that he was somewhere in Dublin. I had almost given up hope when, fifteen minutes before the wedding, he walked into

University Church, gave everybody a big wave and went up to the organist. He sorted out his music in five minutes, and then all we heard from the gallery was his loud, unmistakable, laugh. He had even brought Anthony Kearns, another of the three tenors, along with him. To say the music was excellent would be the understatement of the year.

Our encounters became less frequent as I settled into married life and he went on to become world famous. Shortly after Christmas 2002, I got a call from Ronan. We had not met in two years, but you hardly notice. He was ringing me to wish me a well in the New Year and to congratulate me on my election to Dáil Éireann the previous May. At the end of the call, I asked him what he was doing next. He said he was off to Las Vegas, and I made a joke about Frank Sinatra. After putting down the phone I realised just how appropriate the reference to Sinatra was to Ronan Tynan. To most of us, a disability would often be enough to make us lose confidence; how many of us have talents that we never develop or squander?

That Sinatra song 'I Did It My Way' is what Ronan Tynan is all about. A man who has touched a thousand lives without losing the human touch. Ten thousand words, never mind a thousand words, couldn't say all that I have to say about Ronan; human in many ways like the rest of us, but also a truly inspirational example for all of us.

No Need for a Miracle

Vincent McDonnell

HER NAME IS Joan and she is eight years old. Officially declared to be handicapped, she is about to undertake the greatest adventure of her life. She is going, by herself, on a train journey to Knock. As she waits at Limerick railway station on a sunny summer's morning in 1959, she can hardly believe that when she returns she will no longer be handicapped, but a little girl just like all her friends.

She will have two good legs like all other little girls. The horribly deformed and shortened left limb will have been replaced by a brand new one. Her only worry is that Our Lady, who is going to perform this miracle, will have a perfect match for her good right leg.

She's unsure as to exactly how the miracle will be achieved. Will the bad leg fall off and a new one grow in its place? Even to this eight-year-old, this seems unlikely. What's more likely is that they will have a supply of replacement limbs at Knock and she will be able to choose one for herself. Then it's off with the old one and on with the new. It will simply be like many of the operations she's already had. Only this time there will be no horrible and visible scar to mark the join. She knows Our Lady will never allow that.

As she waits on the platform in her red coat, she feels like the most important person in the world. She does not envy the little girl in a blue dress who is there with her parents

106

seeing someone off. This child wears black patent sandals with silver buckles and her legs above the white ankle socks are smooth and straight and equal in length. But she isn't going to Knock.

Joan knows that her two legs will be exactly like those when she returns. She will no longer have to wear her heavy, black boots, nor the calliper that is attached to the left one. She, too, will be able to wear white ankle socks and patent black sandals with silver buckles. She'll be able to run and play like other children without fear of falling. No longer will she be called Hopalong Cassidy, or cripple, or 'that one with the lame leg'.

The station is crowded, and she holds tight to her father's hand. There are invalids in wheelchairs and on stretchers and others with crutches. She sees a man with a white stick and dark glasses being led by the hand. He is much too big to be that frightened, and she feels proud that she isn't that scared. She lets go her father's hand to show the man how brave she is, but he shuffles past her, his head tilted back as he stares up at the blue sky.

The people in the wheelchairs and the stretchers are loaded on first. At last it is her turn. A steward takes her from her father and helps her on to the train. 'Bye, love,' her father says, his endearment whenever they part. In her eight years there have been many such partings. But this will be the final one. She will not have to go to hospital any more for operations. It will be an end to that – to the parting and the loneliness and the pain.

On the train, a woman takes her hand and leads her to her seat. It's by the window and she looks out, but there is no sign of her father. Panic grips her, and she is about to cry out that she doesn't want to go when he appears at the window. He smiles and winks at her, and she relaxes and realises that she has to go to Knock. Her father wants her to have a new leg, and she can't let him down.

Whistles sound and doors slam. The train jerks and the station begins to move. It's the most amazing sight she has ever seen. While she sits in her seat, the buildings and people whiz past. By the time she's recovered from the shock, her father has slipped by and is lost to sight.

The buildings gather speed, and the moving rails outside the window become a blur. While the train stands still, her father and the railway station and all those people on the platform are heading for Knock. No wonder the train is frantically blowing its whistle. It's being left behind!

It takes a little while for her to realise that in fact the train is moving. Only then does she relax and begin to enjoy the experience. The train picks up speed and starts to sway gently. It goes clickety-clack, clickety-clack, and she thinks that must be its song.

The world outside the window becomes a blur. The dark shapes of trees and poles whiz by at enormous speed. But in the distance, now that they've left the city behind, she can see houses and green fields and cows grazing. A man in a field waves to her. She is tempted to wave back, but she's much too shy.

The blue paper cross, pinned to her coat, declares that she is an invalid. Yet even at eight, Joan detests that word, which she pronounces in-valid and which she's learned at school means 'not any good'. But she knows she is good. She only has polio, a bad leg and a limp. And she wouldn't know she had a limp except that people keep telling her she has one. Sometimes they even demonstrate how she limps. In fact, most of them limp better than she does.

Soon everyone starts saying the rosary. This worries her because she thinks that she might be cured before they reach Knock and she will be put off the train. But when they reach Claremorris, there has been no miracle yet. Here she is put on a bus to take her to Knock. When she arrives there, a steward lifts her down and puts her in a wheelchair. He tucks a blanket firmly about her and hands her into the care of a nurse. This makes Joan uneasy. She's been sent here for a miracle cure, and yet within minutes of arriving finds herself in a wheelchair. It's just as well her mother or father can't see her.

So she's off with Florence Nightingale, attracting what she regards as undeserved sympathetic looks wherever she goes. She attends mass and later, as she's wheeled about the grounds, has gallons of holy water sprinkled on her by elderly women. One lifts up the rug, much to her consternation, and sloshes more holy water on her legs. At the same time, she prays aloud for the poor child to be cured.

Joan is sorely tempted to leap out of the chair and escape. But she knows that if she does so, the woman will drop dead with fright. So she is in a quandary. Here she is at Knock, expecting a new leg, and it seems as if it will take a miracle just to get out of the wheelchair.

The day passes, and she wonders when the miracle is to take place. So far, no one seems to have been cured. Joan asks Florence about the miracle. But she only smiles sadly and pats her on the head. She looks so sad that Joan decides not to ask her again.

Perhaps Our Lady is away in Lourdes, she thinks. Or perhaps they've run out of legs and are awaiting a delivery. But this lack of a miracle doesn't bother Joan any more. Her real worry now is that she might have to keep the wheelchair.

By late afternoon nature takes its course. Joan needs to go to the toilet and Florence wheels her there. Now her eight-year-old sense of decency, coupled with the fact that there is no one here to frighten to death, takes over from her shyness. When Florence takes her arm and says, 'I'll help you in,' Joan thinks to herself, 'Not likely!'

She's up and out of the chair in a flash while Florence stands there astonished. 'My God, you can walk,' she exclaims. Walk! Joan could run if it wasn't for the fact that she's crippled from being confined in the damn chair.

She has a great day in Knock, despite not getting the promised new leg. But after spending so much time in the wheelchair, Joan realises that it wouldn't have been fair to cure her when there were so many other who couldn't walk at all.

More than forty years have passed since that day in Knock, but Joan, my wife, still vividly remembers it. It was the day she was granted the most important miracle of her life – the knowledge that she did not need a miracle at all.

St Patrick's Parade

Senator Feargal Quinn

FOR MANY YEARS St Patrick's Day was a big day for the employees of Superquinn. They didn't work that day, but some four or five hundred of them dressed in their uniforms and joined the Dublin Parade – not just to march, but also to dance and sing!

This took weeks of practice, which everyone enjoyed thoroughly, even though they were not paid to partake. They would gather every Sunday morning in the car park at the Blackrock shop and rehearse. They practised their dance steps – imitating the American high strutters they'd seen the previous year – and they sang their hearts out at those rehearsals.

Then the big day came. Everyone enjoyed an early fun breakfast before donning their uniforms. Butchers, bakers, fishmongers and checkout operators all lined up together in spotless uniforms and with an enthusiasm that shone through that cool mid-March morning. They gathered around St Stephen's Green by nine o'clock, three full hours before the scheduled mid-day start of the parade. The spirit of pride was evident in the faces of everyone who took part, from sixteen-year-olds to sixty-year-olds.

Alongside their dancing colleagues, some of them ran the route giving away hot sausages to some of the half-million crowd who had gathered to see the parade. That was a part of the day that I particularly loved, offering hot sausages to people from around the world and from all walks of life, who welcomed anything that would keep them warm. We always made sure that we kept enough in reserve until we reached the main VIP viewing stand at the GPO in O'Connell Street.

One year I remember jumping on to the stand and offering hot Superquinn pork sausages to all the assembled VIPs – and having them appreciated and devoured by such luminaries as the lord mayor, the taoiseach, the archbishop, etc. – when suddenly I got my first refusal. It was the first time that any one of the 50,000 pork sausages we'd given away had been refused. Surprised that someone had said, 'No', I looked up into the face of a smiling chief rabbi. I think his enjoyment of my mistake was even greater than my embarrassment!

In spite of little setbacks like that, the St Patrick's Day Parade continues to allow us Dubliners to participate with pride in our national holiday.

In Enemy Hands

Anne-Marie Coen

THEY HAD BEEN playing in the garden, all three little girls, with the gate closed and bolted and old Shep, the much loved family dog, on guard, for as a child minder he was second to none and could be relied upon to kick up a rumpus should anything untoward occur. Mrs Kealty had her hands full with a large washing, keeping an eye on the bread baking in the oven and ensuring that the baby continued to sleep for as long as possible by stirring the cradle every now and again to keep it rocking gently and soothingly. But despite her best efforts, he woke suddenly and began howling and yelling with gusto. She picked him up, doing her best to pacify him, but to no avail. There was nothing for it but to sit down, dandle him on her knee and sing to him until the screams abated and his pudgy face became wreathed in smiles. Meanwhile, the bread began to burn and the water grew cold in the washtub.

'Oh, my bread!' She hurriedly returned her youngest child to his cot and attempted to rescue her afternoon's work from ruin. Master James was not best pleased by this cavalier treatment and made his displeasure known. His poor mother didn't know whether she was on her head or her heels in the frenzy of the next few moments. In fact, so distracted did she become that she failed to hear the frantic barking of the sheep dog in the garden, warning of an imminent flight.

The eldest child, a little girl of four, managed to give her jailor the slip and succeeded, with some difficulty, in shooting back the stubborn bolt of the garden gate and now led her two younger siblings out into the wide world of the town, in search of those bad people about whom she had heard her parents talk with both fear and revulsion. The Black and Tans were obviously a people to be dealt with harshly, judging by what her daddy had said. Ensuring that no one was watching from the window, the trio slipped through the gate and toddled off, as fast as their short legs could carry them, in the direction of the main street.

They were very disappointed, for they had come near to the square where Granny and Granddad lived without encountering any of their prey, only old Mr Gibson from next door on his way to the shop, who stopped them and demanded to know if their mammy knew they were out. 'Oh yes,' their captain smiled sweetly, 'she said we could go and visit Granny and Granddad for the afternoon.'

He shook his head deprecatingly. 'I'm surprised at Mrs Kealty, with the way things are an' all.' He looked about him anxiously. 'Well, hurry on over to yeer Gran's house now. It's not safe to be hangin' about the streets these times.'

Ellie assured him that they would, and he went his way, muttering to himself. She didn't, however, lead her little troupe across the street as she had assured her neighbour that she intended to do. As soon as the old man had disappeared into Calloways' for his packet of cigarettes, she led them onwards, down the main street towards the Green, and at last their search was rewarded for, here coming towards them, stepping out in best military fashion, the sun glinting on the barrel of the pistol at his hip, was a fine specimen of their quarry. They stopped and subjected the Auxiliary to a sharp scrutiny before approaching and encircling him, rather in the manner of an ambush. He looked down on them from his great height and, to their surprise, smiled and spoke quite pleasantly.

'Hello, little girls,' he said, 'and what are you doing out alone? Don't you know it's very dangerous to be out and about without your mama?'

'Yes, we do know. Mammy and Daddy told us all about the Black and Tans, and that's why we sneaked away from home. We want to catch them and kill them.' Ellie formed her small hand into the shape of a minute pistol and pointed it at the officer. 'I'm going to shoot you, you dirty Black and Tan! Bang, bang. Bang, bang, bang, bang, bang!'

'Who are you and where do you live?' this invincible member of the enemy demanded of the tiny rebel.

'I'm Ellie Kealty, and I live up there,' she pointed back in the direction in which she and her co-conspirators had come.

'Well, you come with me!' and before the defiant infant had time to raise any objections, she found herself caught firmly by the arm and being led in the direction of her home, protesting strongly against such treatment. The other two, by now hot and tired and longing for the security of their mother's arms, began to wail dolefully.

People came to their doors to see what the cause of the commotion was and, discovering its source, hurried back inside, crossed themselves, and locked and bolted their homes against invasion. 'Oh, God have mercy on them, the little craturs, and their poor parents!' was the desperate prayer they uttered.

Mrs Kealty, the baby in her arms, her bread rescued from incineration, was just about to call her three eldest in from the garden to be washed and fed when a loud tattoo fell on the door. 'Glory be to God, who could that be?' she gasped, fear evident in her clear, grey eyes. She ran into the front room where her husband sat cross-legged on his bench, sewing diligently, and peeped through the window in the direction of the front door.

'Oh, my God, Ned, it's one of them, it's one of the Black and Tans. They know, they must know! I told you it was too dangerous, especially with the children in the house! You know the kind those people are!'

'Shh, Helen, shh. We don't know what he wants. Just let him in and carry on as normal. Bring him into the kitchen. Offer him tea, or something stronger, and keep him there until—'. But before he could finish, the front door opened and the officer of the Auxiliaries, leading the still-protesting Ellie and followed by the howling duo, came into the hall, and seeing the young mother, babe in arms, standing in the doorway of her husband's sewing room, approached her, and pushed the eldest Kealty towards her.

'I beg pardon, ma'am, for entering your house uninvited, but I have been knocking for quite some time without receiving any reply, and these children are becoming more and more distressed and in need of their mother. I have to say, ma'am, that I was very surprised to find them wandering the streets unattended, especially in the present political climate, and as for walking up to members of the Auxiliary Forces and threatening to shoot them! Well, I'm afraid most of my men would not appreciate the sentiment!

'As I am sure you are only too well aware, even the lives of children are not sacred to many of them. Please explain this to your little ones as best you can, and for pity's sake keep them off the streets. It is extremely dangerous out there, especially now, with this escaped insurgent on the loose!' He paused. If he had noticed the scared look in the woman's eyes or her sidelong glances in the direction of the bench on which her husband sat, or if he had heard the sneeze, hastily smothered, which seemed to come from the vicinity of beneath the same bench, he showed no sign of it. He merely apologised once more for having burst in unannounced and took his leave of the relieved, yet perplexed family.

A figure emerged from beneath the tailor's worktop and stretched. 'By God, that was a close one an' no mistake!' the soldier of the Republic exclaimed, letting out his breath in a long, low whistle. The young mother hugged her children and thanked the Lord for at least one officer and gentleman among *Na Sasanaigh*.

That Was Long Ago and This Is Now

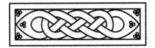

Robert Jordan

B ARRY WAS OUR eldest child, born just nine months and two weeks after we got married. He was tall, very tall, finishing up at 6ft 7in. He loved his hugs, and when he would return at weekends from college, his first requirement was a lengthy hug from his mom especially, but also from me. As he grew he became very independent in certain respects, although he always retained an extremely close relationship with his mother. One day he solemnly announced to her that he wouldn't need as many hugs as before, as he had met a girl, Róisín. One way his independence showed was in his refusal to join in if we were having what I call a *bitching session,* giving out about someone. He used to say, 'You can't criticise till you have walked in their shoes.'

One Sunday we came home from a few days in Donegal to find the house in turmoil. Barry had almost finished his final exams with just one project to submit by the following Friday. He went out to a party only to discover, halfway through, that he had get his dates wrong; the project had to be in by Monday, not Friday, so instead of seven days, he had just three.

In a mad panic he spent the weekend, with his brother's assistance, researching, writing and typing his project. Everything went wrong: the computer crashed, the printer wouldn't work, he had the wrong textbook, the files he copied in college were incompatible with our home computer. It seemed that Murphy's Law went into full operation: if it could go wrong, it did. In the event, he submitted his work, none too beautifully presented, in time, and went to his girlfriend's house where they spent a long time talking and drinking, 'as you do', to use his own phrase.

The following day, Barry complained of a headache, which became more severe as the day went on. Paracetamol tablets and sleep seemed the most obvious solution, but he didn't sleep long, and when he awoke his head was throbbing with unbearable pain. The doctor told us he was concerned about the possibility of meningitis, but in hospital it turned out that he had developed a blood infection, causing a clot under his brain. Within twenty-four hours he was blind in his right eye, and despite constant, round-the-clock efforts and observations by the medical and nursing staff, Barry died after twelve days, aged just twenty-one years. Fifteen hundred people came to his funeral.

Incidentally, he passed his exams, but the only time his name bore his 'letters' was in his death notice in the newspaper. At the graduation, one of his tutors gave us the text of a poem he had written as part of his 'Computers in Society' course:

> *In the world long ago, we, the people, believed in God,*
> *And the word of the Church was as good as God, or so we thought.*
> *We were ignorant of the world and ignorant of our ignorance.*
> *That was long ago and this is now, and the world is a very different place.*
> *In the world long ago, the trusted men of the church*
> *Broke the rules and were caught, and the sceptics felt great.*

*But our worldview was destroyed and we knew not
    what to think.*
*The powerful were humbled, but uncertainty reigned
    and we were confused.*
*That was long ago and this is now and the world is
    a very different place.*
In the world long ago, we needed something to do.
The men (and women) of science proposed a way,
*And we let them free to tell us of the world we lived
    in and why we existed.*
*That was long ago and this is now and the world is
    a very different place.*
*In the world long ago, we got tired of waiting for
    answers,*
And so we made ourselves comfortable.
*We built technologies to help improve our world and
    we were successful,*
*And the quality of life quickly became such that the
    need to work became questionable.*
*There was a need for work to be done, but our tech-
    nologies could do most, and it was good.*
*In the world long ago, the meaning of life came into
    question.*
*Was it to gather wealth? To get a job? To intoxicate
    ourselves?*
*It once had seemed so to many, but there was little
    true joy.*
*But we found another way; a way that gave our free
    time meaning:*
Friends became the most important thing,
*And our interaction with them and the world, so
    long neglected, filled us.*
That was not so long ago, now that I think of it.

In a footnote, he added, 'This is written from a perspective that is present, but not yet, and may not ever occur. It is

an attempt to show the possible place of computers and their related technologies in the context of the evolution of humans up to now and an evolution of humans from now on into the third millennium.'

It is a thought.

Thirty-Five Years A-Changing

Lorna Roberts

IT WAS IN 1966 that I fell in love with Connemara. Being a great fan of The Bachelors, I was inspired by Dec Cluskey's eloquent description of his visits to the Gaeltacht area of Connemara. This was over thirty-five years ago when only a few people in the West of Ireland had cars, televisions and telephones; there was time to chat and enjoy each other's company and a quality of life that is disappearing.

The following year I was left the grand sum of £200 by a ninety-nine-year-old aunt. I often wish that I could tell her how I spent that money; little did she know that it was to change my life.

'What will you do with it?' they all asked.

'I'll buy an old stone ruin in Connemara!' was my reply.

'She's mad of course,' I heard them say.

£200 was a lot of money in the late sixties before decimalisation caused prices to soar, so I was overjoyed when I met Annie, who led me to Emlagharan, the most beautiful spot on this planet, and told me that she was selling plots – for £200. I was sure that fate had brought me here, so without hesitation Annie and I went to the solicitor and the deal was done.

Fortunately I was neither old enough nor wise enough to think beyond the dream, or I might have anticipated the difficulties and had cold feet. Instead I went post-haste to my bank manager. Perhaps the fact that his name was Denys O'Brien helped. Although he had never been to Ireland, he was intrigued and interested.

'Yes, I'll lend you £1,000 on one condition – that you keep me informed of how the building progresses, send photographs, and if at the end of the summer you have £1,000 worth of house, I'll lend you more. If you haven't, don't ever come near this bank again!'

That was a sound philosophy and presented itself as a challenge, which resulted in all my friends being called up to spend their college holidays on a building site. We camped in two caravans – one for the boys and one for the girls. Life was 'proper' in those days, but firm friendships were established, and we are now all godparents to each other's children. That building site has a lot to answer for as it has resulted in two successful marriages, four children and two grandchildren – so far!

Life was simple. The only cooking was done on two Calor gas rings, and all water had to be collected from a lake fifty yards below. Was it chance that two of us were Aquarians? As water bearers it was our job to carry all the water from the lake. Was it also chance that my boyfriend at the time was the chef in the best hotel in town? Those rare dinners out were very special. Our other moments away from the building site were spent in a local bar that doubled as builders' merchants, so all the buying of materials was done over the bar at night. That was useful as time was limited, so we didn't waste precious daylight hours.

The house was built in sixteen weeks, in four sessions spread over eighteen months. It was fun, rewarding and created a great deal of local interest. The only people who built holiday houses at that time were the wealthy, who paid a builder to get on with it. This mad crowd were doing it with the guidance of the *Readers' Digest* building manual, a lot of advice from Eamonn who owned the pub and the combined

skills of John, my brother, who had learnt building construction as part of a surveying course, Bob, an engineer, and
Paul, who had done odd jobs on building sites. People visited every day, bringing vegetables, eggs and plenty of advice.
In return we had parties. The Guinness flowed, and I am told
that the fact that so many Guinness bottles were thrown into
the foundations is the reason that the rats stayed away. The
music drifted into the early hours, as everyone arrived with
fiddles, accordions and some haunting local songs. My
friendly chef produced Irish coffee in tumblers, so the singing
went on till dawn.

My brother had a fish business in England, and during
those building days he had spent many happy hours chatting
to local fishermen. He was horrified to hear that there were
no markets and turbot was being thrown back into the sea
because they couldn't sell it. John made some enquiries,
decided that he would move his family to Connemara and
build a fish factory beside the harbour.

The house was now built, but it had involved a few more
visits to the bank manager. He was fascinated by the whole
project, but was a little taken aback twelve years later when
I said that I needed to borrow again as I was going to start
a restaurant in the house, which would involve building an
extension and putting in electricity. He showered me with
good advice, telling me that everyone loses money in the
catering business. 'But I know that you will do it anyway,' he
said, and lent me the money.

I had spent several years as a children's hostess aboard a
cruise ship and long happy summers in Connemara working
at local hotels. It was then that it dawned on me that there
was a need for a middle-of-the-road restaurant. By combin-
ing my experience in the tourist business, a brother providing local fish and a house with one of the best views in
Connemara, overlooking an eighteen-hole golf course, the
ingredients for a restaurant emerged.

I opened *Mainly Seafood,* a simple, inexpensive restaurant serving hungry tourists, sitting at tables cramped together in my homemade house. The windows creaked, the turf fire burned, the food was fresh and locally produced, and they loved it. My dream home had suddenly become the fashionable place to eat, as we entertained musicians, artists, film stars, politicians and visitors from every corner of the globe from Alaska to Borneo. We watched anxiously every night as well-wined drivers of Mercedes and BMWs left in the early hours to negotiate a mile of dirt track that skirted a deep lake. Amazingly no one ever went in that lake. I am told that the mother of the late, great Brian Lenihan insisted that all her friends should eat at Emlagharan to experience the drive home!

Now there are so many restaurants in Connemara that we are no longer unique, and Emlagharan has become a house again with happy and varied memories.

There have been many changes. The pace of life today allows little time for storytelling and the *craic.* Expensive cars accompany the new designer homes, and every house has a telephone and television. These are material changes, but the place is as beautiful as ever, and even if progress has changed so much of Connemara in thirty-five years, the magic is still there, the beaches are clean and empty, the mountains dark and mysterious, and the colours intense. It was the colours and lights that inspired me to write a book, *Colourful Connemara,* which I took to 4,000 travel agents all over Europe. After a particularly bad tourist season in 1992, everyone murmured, 'Why doesn't somebody do something?' so I did! I produced the book in five different languages and headed off with it to all the major cities on the Continent.

The Dubliners frequently visit Connemara, and it was after a music session in my house, following one of their concerts, that John Sheahan wrote 'The Connemara Sunrise', a beautiful piece of music, which he contributed to my book. Anyone who experiences a Connemara sunrise, a Connemara sunset, and the hours between, has surely lived life to the full.

Hiroshima – an Irish Survivor

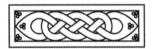

John Edward 'Ed' Murphy

ON THE MORNING of 6 August 1945, an American B-29 superfortress bomber, the *Enola Gay,* flew 31,000 feet over the Japanese city of Hiroshima and dropped a 9,000-pound atomic bomb. The bomb accelerated the end of World War II, but the human cost was frightful. People were burned and maimed, and it is estimated that at least 100,000 died that day or in the immediate aftermath. More were to die over the ensuing years from various illnesses attributed to radiation exposure.

Unknown to most of the world, an Irish nun, Sister Mary of St Isaac Joques, survived the attack and subsequently provided aid and assistance to many of its victims. But how did an Irish citizen find herself in Hiroshima on that fateful day?

The story starts over half a century earlier, in November 1893, when Catherine Canny gave birth to her third child. Christened Julia, she was brought up on their modest farm in Upper Kilbeg near Clonbur in County Galway. (Amazingly, over a hundred years later, the farm still exists, and the last I heard, it was being operated by Julia's great-nephew, Steve Canny.)

Following the lead of older brother Stephen and in the footsteps of many of her contemporaries, Julia left her home in 1921 and emigrated to America. But sometime before her departure, she had seen an article in a magazine asking for vocations to the missions. Although she didn't fully realise it at the time, a new flame was ignited by that article; a flame that would burn brightly for the rest of her life.

Landing in the new world, Julia lived with Stephen and his family in New Jersey, very close to New York City. For a time she had a job doing domestic and housekeeping duties for a nearby medical facility. However, Stephen's daughter, Clare, remembers Julia as a beautiful seamstress and thinks that she may also have worked in that occupation in the New York garment industry.

Julia's secular life came to an end on 21 November 1931, when the flame was reignited and she entered the novitiate for the Society of the Helpers at Chappaqua, just outside New York City. On that day Julia – the name – vanished to be replaced by Sr Mary of St Isaac Joques, in honour of the Canadian Jesuit missionary who was martyred in 1646.

Shortly after entering the Helpers, Sr Isaac expressed her long-standing desire to work in the overseas missions. During a 1985 interview with Irish journalist Adrian Miller, she said, 'Of course, we weren't permitted to speak in those days, so I just dropped the slip of paper in the Superior's box.' Her request remained unanswered for eight years until 1939, when she gleefully accepted an assignment to the Helpers' convent in Hiroshima, which was dedicated to operating a mission and school.

Sr Isaac arrived just five days before Christmas and threw herself into her work with a genuine enthusiasm. One of the convent's residents was a twenty-two-year old novice, Sr Theresia Yamada, who remembered Julia as kindly, hard working, and liked by the community. She was big and strong with very bright blue eyes, and Sr Theresia particularly remembered her pleasing smile. Sr Isaac made her perpetual vows during the summer of 1940 at a pontifical mass cele-brated by the Bishop of Hiroshima in the city's cathedral, with Sr Theresia and other members of the Helpers in attendance.

Less than eighteen months later, America and Japan went to war, and the Japanese authorities interned Sr Isaac, thinking she was an American. Fortunately, after about seven months, the authorities discovered she was an Irish citizen – a neutral alien – and released her.

As the *Enola Gay* arrived six miles above the city, ready to unleash it's deadly weapon, the sisters had just completed celebrating mass. The celebrant was a German Jesuit, Fr Coops, from the nearby Jesuit Novitiate at Nagatsuki.

The bomb detonated at 8.16 a.m., less than one and a half miles from the convent, levelling everything and killing tens of thousands for several miles around. What follows is Sr Isaac's description of the atomic bomb blast as told to Adrian Miller and published in the Belfast *Andersontown News*.

> *Suddenly there was a huge bang in the sky, just above the city. We were all thrown from our seats onto the ground. Realising that it was a bomb, we quickly picked ourselves up and made a run for cover in the direction of the convent. We had only just taken shelter inside the convent when the entire building began to shake and give way. We turned and rushed outside again, the convent collapsing at our heels. The convent wall collapsed before our very eyes and beyond where the wall had stood until a few seconds before lay the remains of our neighbourhood. There was hardly a building left standing. Everywhere people lay either dying or dead, burned – I was to learn later – from the flash of radiation.*

When they ran for cover, the sisters did not realise the importance of their action, but they had taken shelter in the convent for the few seconds it took the fiery flash of radiation to sweep past – the same force that subsequently destroyed the convent – and as a result they survived the initial blast. With so much devastation and death all around them, Sr Isaac attributed their survival to a miracle.

Fr Coops directed the sisters to move away from the now destroyed convent. Fires were fast approaching, and he urged them to seek refuge at the Jesuit novitiate about six miles away in Nagatsuki where the director was Fr Pedro Arrupe, later to become director general of the Jesuits. The journey to Nagatsuki was frequently interrupted, as Sr Isaac and her colleagues ignored their own plight and stopped to provide aid, comfort, and assistance to other refugees – all homeless and hungry, stunned and disoriented, many sick or injured, and many seriously burned.

After an arduous journey, the sisters arrived at Nagatsuki where they found refuge with some ninety injured and burned refugees. The sisters worked with the Jesuits, providing shelter, food, emergency medical assistance and spiritual support – both to the refugees already in the residence and in the nearby areas. Sr Theresia confirmed that only three of the ninety refugees died. This relatively small attrition rate is a great testimony to the unceasing work of the caregivers.

In Nagatsuki, Sr Isaac and a Jesuit brother, Masui, were given the overwhelming task of finding and distributing food to the refugees. It is a task she must have developed an appetite for, because finding and distributing food became her calling during the post-war era as well.

Over the ensuing months, occupation troops began to arrive in Hiroshima. Some of the American and Australian troops were of Irish descent, and Sr Isaac found that her knowledge of English – not to mention her lilting Galway brogue – went far in providing for the sisters and the children from their convent school. She later said, 'I became the Society's beggar!'

Sr Isaac spent the remainder of her life in Japan, but continued to maintain contact by mail with her extended family in Ireland and America. She died in Tokyo on 1 November 1987, just nine days short of her ninety-fourth birthday, on the Feast of All Saints, a date of considerable importance to her order, the Society of Helpers of the Holy Souls.

Two years earlier, at the conclusion of his interview, Adrian Miller said, 'As I made my way back out through the convent, I could hear a voice cry loud and clear *"Slán agus beannacht"*. In the course of nearly 50 years, Sister Isaac may never have mastered the Japanese language, but neither had Julia quite forgotten her Irish. Indeed, I began to doubt whether in 1921 Julia had really left Ireland behind at all. Had she not rather, brought it with her?'

The TD's Clinic

Liz McManus TD

Once more I leave the well-lit streets,
The shopping arcades and human company.
Only my car lights peer ahead, isolate a gorse
Bush on the roadside and the dark's menace.

As I burrow under the quilt of night a voice
On the radio tells me this monthly ritual is dying,
Its demise prescribed by telephone, email and
Loss of patronage. People are wiser now,

They can read and write, stand up for themselves.
Maybe. But if true, the news hasn't reached
My destination. In the hotel at Killagarvey
People are waiting for a peddler of wares

With a briefcase and overcoat; a gatekeeper
To another world where the rules are made
And the barriers built. Those who can afford it
Have a drink at the bar. Those who can't

Sit. I know each one or I soon will. Our fastrack
Trade in medical cards, headage payments, a dying
Wife or planning permission will see to that.
Because they vote they own me. Even when they

Don't vote I see myself as giver. Then my hand is
Clasped and a frayed sleeve and shirred thumbnail
Makes intimate another's life; its laments; auguries,
Signs and secret joys; its gift of country warmth.

The Son of My Father

Kevin Kelly

IT WAS NINE o'clock on a cold winter's evening in the West of Ireland. My parents had just put in their regular twelve-hour shift at our petrol station. Now, it was time for rest. On my way home from work, I joined them for a quick cup of tea. Given the time, it was easy to picture the scene that awaited me. My father's whereabouts were fairly predictable. At around a quarter past nine every evening, one could expect to find him sitting with his feet up beside a blazing open fire. With the paper in one hand and a cup of tea in the other, he was ready to unwind!

And so it was.

Two cream crackers lushly covered in butter and marmalade were within arm's reach. Either the radio, which was strategically placed beside the prayer book to his right hand side, or the TV, in the corner to his left, would provide additional entertainment. His own perfect pleasure station.

In this zone, happiness prevailed.

There was better than this, I was convinced.

Having successfully broken into the consultancy market, I found contentment in consumerism. In contrast, my father, though a very successful and generous person, chose not to surround himself with the all-important trappings. This puzzled me. Whereas my father chose to have only two suits – one for work, the other for very special occasions – I had the full range! While my father enjoyed his time-outs, I had no time to waste. Every moment was precious. We appeared worlds apart. Why were we so different? Violating the prevailing calm, I decided to investigate.

'Daddy, why don't you go out and buy a few new suits?' I enquired. Choosing to reserve comment, my father smiled, redirecting his attention to the paper. 'Was the student not ready?' I wondered

Two years later, I started to travel extensively. Each journey presented a new lesson to integrate. During my visit to Tibet, my travels took me to its capital Lhasa. Before exploring the locality, the services of a driver, Bimpka, and a translator, Pasang, were secured. An itinerary, which included visiting all the important Tibetan holy sites and discussions with different families, was agreed upon. This, I hoped, would give me a greater insight into the Tibetan way.

On the way to Samye Monastery, Tibet's first monastery, unwilling to let this opportunity pass, I canvassed Bimpka for his thoughts on life. 'Bimpka, I want you to imagine that a fairy godmother appears and will give you anything you want, anything at all. What would you request?'

Having travelled with him for three days, I could readily have compiled a customised wish list on his behalf. For a start, he needed a thumb and another finger to accompany the lonely three on his left hand. Then I reflected on the agony and suffering I experienced while travelling cross-country, overland from the Kathmandu border town of Kodari to Shigatse. I remember vividly thinking death was nigh, such were the ill effects of the journey. Cold sweat was dripping down my back in rhythm with the many waterfalls, and my forehead was like an oven. Going in and out of large gorges for 120km wasn't fun, but how could I justify complaining? Bimpka did this type of journey every day. Maybe an aeroplane or a new ultra-deluxe four-wheel drive car will feature on his wish list, I thought.

'What would I want? Haven't I got all that I need?' Bimpka exclaimed as he looked at me quizzically, then burst out laughing.

'What?' I screamed internally. 'Surely you want at least two fingers.'

'Are you sure?' I pressed.

'Yes!' he replied calmly and with the quiet confidence that comes from knowing oneself within.

He didn't need anything. He was happy with his lot. Shocked, I began to appreciate the significance of my father's unspoken wisdom. It appeared that oftentimes, important lessons were caught, not taught.

'Had I travelled around the world to integrate some home truths?' I pondered.

Bimpka and my dad appeared to have much in common. Both were happy with their lot. Simplicity reigned. It appeared that nothing in the outside world was likely to change their state of mind. They obviously found contentment by living inside out rather than outside in.

On my return I spent some time with my father exploring his philosophy on life. It turns out that my grandfather was also a businessman, and he also owned two suits – one for the first six days of the week and a Sunday best.

'On Saturday evening, everybody would meticulously prepare their clothes for mass the following morning. Shoes would be polished, shirts ironed and suits pressed. Every Sunday, from dawn to dusk, your grandfather was immaculately turned out, in his suit and his Christie hat. The emphasis in our home was on the quality of the person, not on the quality and quantity of his clothes. We didn't need to buy a new suit to become a new person,' my father informed me.

On reflection, one couldn't but appreciate this wisdom. Yet I, the student, wasn't ready, subconsciously choosing to pay little more than lip service to those insights.

A year later, I committed to following my bliss, to pursuing a professional speaking career in the area of personal excellence. This involved giving up my lucrative consultancy career, but more significantly resulted in a change of status. I went from high income to near no income in a very short space of time.

Simple economics dictated that trappings were a luxury I could ill-afford. A clearout was required to balance the books. Though painful at the start, I know now that it was the catalyst for some amazing personal growth. Less junk to distract allowed more time to reflect. Without these outside distractions, the more my inner whispers propelled me forward. By starting to intuit, I was truly honouring my Celtic ancestors.

Pain was obviously the greatest architect of all time. It shaped and moulded me into a better person. My father's homespun wisdom began to permeate my soul. Happiness was now to be found in simple pleasures. Watching the waves, smelling the flowers or enjoying the sweetness of silence all fired my soul.

My contentment had turned to joy as life weaved its magic over me.

It appeared that the torch had finally been passed on to the next generation.

I was fast becoming the son of my father

Where will I be at quarter past nine in the evening in twenty-five years time?

Naked Truths

Áine Greaney

IT HAD JUST turned 1970. For Ireland, this would be the decade of the European Union, the era of Gary Glitter, the Brady Bunch and Joe Dolan. But on this winter afternoon, our little country classroom has bigger productions at stake. There we are, a chorus line of seven- and eight-year-old girls, all singing our hearts out in preparation for next week's school concert. Our *pièce de theâtre* is a fetching little lullaby in which we cradle and rock our imaginary babies. The chorus, if memory serves me, went something like this:

> *Rocking my baby, I'll rock her to sleep*
> *And over her slumber a watch I will keep*
> *I'm happy my baby to rock you, you see*
> *I'm bound to rock you as my mother rocked me.*

This last line rises to an emphatic crescendo as our cardiganed elbows jab toward the ceiling.

That four-teacher school had green walls and high windows, classrooms that smelled of dust and drenched, muddy floorboards. Beyond the windows was the tarmacadam playground that was bordered by stone walls and fields.

Inside those windows we recited morning prayers, grace before meals, multiplication tables and spellings. Every morning we stood around a nylon board with cartoon pictures of our Irish *comhrá* (conversation) lessons. Yes, Ireland might be entering the disco era, but the notion of child-centered education, or child-centred anything for that matter, was still light years away.

Take Two. We are finished with today's practice. But before we toddle back to our desk rows, our teacher warn us to have our props ready tomorrow: next week, those red stage curtains will open. And there, in that drafty village hall, our parents and everyone else in the parish would sit huddled in their tubular chairs and munching their Liquorice Allsorts or their Green Oatfield toffees. Waiting for us to entertain them. Tomorrow, we were each to bring our dolls to school. We were to be choreographed and ready to sing and rock them to sleep.

Was I the only little girl with a secret? Probably not. But mine had imminent consequences and was definitely the most sinful.

I had a doll – a gift from Santa Claus that previous Christmas – but bringing her into school, into this co-ed classroom, was out of the question. For here was my secret: at home I had hidden my naked doll in an old wardrobe where we kept winter coats and wellingtons and work boots. Sometimes the dog slept there. She lay on the top shelf, face down with her little pink buttocks peeping from between the old woollen caps and scarves. Starkers. In her birthday suit. In the nip – the source of all my seven-year-old shame and insomnia.

Like her predecessors, she had stared back at me from that cellophane fronted box on Christmas morning – a stilt-ed perfection of nylon hair and curling lashes and a crino-line dress. But long before our New Year and the new decade, I had dismantled all that perfection, convinced, as always, that Santa Claus hadn't a clue about dressmaking. I could design and make something far superior and cer-tainly far groovier. And so I spent that Christmas holiday, as I had others, drawing fashion designs on the backs of

Christmas cards, waiting to sneak the household scissors from the kitchen drawer and gauging my grandmother's moods for when I could cadge a sewing needle.

But Christmas is long gone now, and all my couture designs and cutouts lie scattered about the house. And as for that original, crinoline dress? It has either been lost or the dog has chewed it. Meanwhile, I, and I alone, know of my doll's secret hideout and her shameful state of dishabille.

By this age I have been privy to some whispered titbits, but I still have no verifiable evidence of where babies come from and know little of birds or bees or carnal knowledge. But I know that those naked little buttocks and that dimpled belly button controvert what my grandmother calls *modesty.* 'Be modest,' she would entreat us girls. 'Always be modest in word and deed.'

Here we are, the following afternoon, and it's concert practice again. And there's our ragged little chorus line, ponytails and pigtails and severely cut fringes, and all of us cradling our dolls and ready to rock and rock around the clock.

The teacher gives me a little frown. 'And where's yours?'

Cheeks burning. Eyes stinging. 'I – I forgot.'

There's that lipstick smile of hers. 'Tomorrow. Don't forget tomorrow.'

She is an unusually kind woman, a lady of make-up and perfumes and A-line skirts.

Relief. I have bought myself another night. Like every con artist, time is everything to me now. But that evening and the next few evenings my dressmaking plans go badly awry. And how to cut and fit and sew without unearthing her nakedness from that dark wardrobe? Toward the end of the week, the teacher furrows her brow, purses her lips at me. She means business. My last chance. Show must go on. That doll of mine better be in tomorrow.

That evening, I sneak the doll from her hiding place and

swaddle her in an old, frayed dish cloth, then hide her among the books in my school bag. Another sleepless night, when I shut my eyes and pray for sleep, but see only my classmates' faces – especially the boys – freckled, laughing, leering. And did I deserve any better? I am an immodest girl. A liar. A hoarder of naked bodies and squalid secrets.

'*Na bábóga* (the dolls),' the teacher prompts us. The other girls cross to the hearth and the painted mantel where all week the stage dolls stand lined up and ready.

Take my place in the line. Don't look left or right.

Teacher leads us in. We are singing, rocking our babies, rock them to sleep. Rocking our little pink doll faces and blue eyes and fluffy little dresses and . . . my doll's bare legs peeping from under the tea-stained dish cloth. Cheeks burning. My lips and mouth mimicking the words – *I'm bound to rock you as my mother rocked me* – but my mind galloping, racing for miles and miles and miles.

There! She's looking at me now. Turquoise eye shadow and her teacher's eyes agape at the sight of the dishcloth.

She looks away again. Inscrutable.

Eons later, on another planet on another galaxy, that day's practice is finally over. We all turn back to the mantel where we stow our dolls in readiness for tomorrow. And there's mine, the ragged, dishcloth hobo among the beauty queens.

For the rest of that afternoon we are assigned to work quietly on our writing and maths. Heads down, erasers squeaking across the pages, whispers and notes passed when we think she's not looking.

They say that the families of tragedy, those who wait by a phone or pace a hospital waiting room, can deny the most irrefutable truths. They can concoct, fabricate: a medical miracle will happen. The long-missing child will walk through that door.

But that afternoon in that old, country classroom, I learned that it can be same with good news. The evidence is before our eyes, yet we cannot, dare not believe. Don't seize the moment or leap with joy. Deny the outlandish but delightful possibility of deliverance.

From my writing workbook I sneak glances at her – first rummaging in her sewing cupboard, then sitting behind her teacher's table, her pink lips drawn together in concentration. She cuts, she pins, eyes narrowed as she threads the needle.

Three o'clock. At last she looks up from her work, bids us to stand for evening prayers. We scrape back our chairs and bless ourselves and chant in unison. Bless ourselves again and jostle, race for the door.

Except me.

I am summoned to her table.

And there it is: the green, tartan doll poncho with fringed edges, stitched with matching green thread. The little skirt has a tiny safety pin in imitation of a Scottish kilt. I retrieve my doll from the mantel. We dress her together. She warns that this outfit is to be left alone now. Left intact.

In the years afterward we would learn all about birds and bees and boys and babies and what immodesty really meant. We would learn composition, percentages, history of Ireland, and geography of the thirty-two counties. But that little doll kilt and matching poncho was my first lesson; my first encounter with sweet, sudden kindness.

Christmas Redemption

Sean Lyons

I WORKED AS a teacher in Zambia in the eighties. I was based in a small village, where there was poverty in the material sense but there was, I felt, contentment. My first Christmas there, I was invited to spend the holiday with a priest friend of mine in one of the cities in the industrialised area known as the Copper Belt.

He wrote and told me he would collect me at the railway station in the city at 7 p.m. on Christmas Eve. To get from my village took two days by bus and train. On the journey, I was robbed at a bus station, and the train taking me the final leg of the journey broke down. I arrived in the city shortly before midnight Christmas Eve, broke, tired and miserable. My friend had given up waiting for me. His address and contact number were in my stolen wallet, so I was stranded.

Leaving the train station, I stepped into a scene from a nightmare. The mines had closed for the holiday, so the street was filled with a mob of drunken, celebrating revellers. I could see at least two fistfights in progress, and several men lay bleeding on the ground. There was even an occasional burst of gunfire.

Up the street, there stood a hotel. Music blared from the bar, and prostitutes and their clients swarmed at the doorway. More in hope than anything else, I went to the hotel to see if a room was available. A giant of a barman shook his head and, in a surprisingly kind voice, suggested that a young white man might not be safe around there. When I asked if a taxi was possible, he just smiled and went back to work.

I stood outside the door. It was approaching midnight. Soon, it would be Christmas, and I was far from home, lost, frightened and very alone. A prostitute came over to me and asked if I was in trouble. Her voice was soft, and I could barely speak, so touched was I by her kindness. She gave me a hug and told me to wait a moment. She left me there and came back a little while later with what I can only describe as one of the most frightening looking men I have ever seen. He was not tall but was broad and muscular. His shaved head was scarred, and his face was pock-marked from childhood smallpox. His eyes were bloodshot and hard looking.

'Come with us,' the young woman said. 'We will bring you somewhere safe.'

She took my hand and led me through the crowd. The presence of her bald friend meant we were allowed through. We came to a small car, and he opened the door and gestured for me to get in. We drove away from the noise and violence into a quiet suburb and parked outside a small church.

'There are Irish priests here, maybe they know your friend,' she said. I knew she was anxious for me to leave so she could get back to plying her trade, and so I shook both of her hands and bade her farewell. The driver grunted impatiently. As I left, she leaned out the window and bade me the traditional goodbye: 'Travel well, my friend.'

I met my priest friend soon after and told him of my adventures. I have had many adventures since, and I have travelled well since. I often think of the woman who offered me redemption that dark Christmas night. Since that time Aids has ravaged the beautiful country of Zambia. One of the victims was the son of the then president, Kenneth Kaunda. Mr Kaunda has bravely spoken publicly about his son's death, hoping to spare others his fate. Aids has infected nearly 100 per cent of the sex workers in Zambia, the overwhelming majority driven into the life to feed impoverished families.

I have no doubt my caring and inspiring friend is dead, the victim of the tortuous plagues of poverty, inequality and disease. I often think of her and her humanity and kindness. Every Christmas, I light a candle for her. My journey continues. The hope and optimism I learned during my idyllic youth in the West of Ireland has been reinforced many times but never more fundamentally than by the outcast, downtrodden, unfortunate, loving woman in one of the roughest quarters of Africa.

A Witness to History

Mary Kenny

MRS KATHLEEN MURPHY was born Kathleen Donnellan in Oughterard, County Galway, in January 1906, and she lives in Loughrea County Galway in 2003. She can remember the early years of the twentieth century with sparkling clarity.

'The people at that time spoke Irish not English in Oughterard,' she recalls. 'My father was a native Irish speaker. My aunt (by marriage) wasn't able to speak any English. 'Twas all Irish. She would have been born in the 1850s.

'As well as being a teacher my father was a correspondent for the Associated Press, and he did an awful lot of travelling. He wrote about the Maamtrasna murders in 1882. I was about eleven when he died.' Her father was William J Donnellan, and she believes he died of tuberculosis, as many did at that time. 'He was a very vain man. He could have been a well-off man; he went into the courts and interpreted from Irish. He did all that work and the only reward was "Would you come in for a half one?" (a half pint). He never got a fee at all.' Times were hard after her father died – leaving four children.

'We were very poor, extremely poor. My mother was left destitute. At that time, people were expected to live on air when their breadwinner died. No relief of any kind, although the pension came in 1909. They were making up songs about it.'

> *Five shillings is the pension, it was granted by the*
> *State*
> *To keep the old and feeble from outside the work-*
> *house gate.*

'It was greatly welcome. There were an awful lot of beggarmen around the place in those days. Poor men, and poor women as well, going to officer to get a rent ticket to sleep in the workhouse.'

Kathleen's mother, Delia, was an enterprising woman, and she managed to get a job as caretaker at the Courthouse. 'She was paid for that. She got the fuel fee and things like that. And we set the house – the house was our own. And we had the little bit of land. But that didn't make out an awful lot, I'll tell you. So 'twas hard.

'And yet I don't remember a lot about hardship, because she never let me know. There was no such thing as going hungry. But the food was very plain, let me tell you. I had a very good aunt who was a great dressmaker, and she supplied me with clothes. She really made my Communion frocks, and my Confirmation, you know, all that kind of thing.' Shoes were the greatest expense for a family at that time, although the children in Connemara would always go barefoot in the summer time, which Kathleen relished. To this day, she has scarcely a corn or a bunion on her feet.

To listen to Kathleen remembering times gone by is to be brought back to the early days of the twentieth century, now a part of history; and Kathleen tells a story like the *seanchaí* used to do.

'I'll tell you a little story about how I heard of the insurrection of 1916.

'My father always got the newspaper which people didn't always get in those days. He got the *Freeman's Journal*. He was a Parnellite, and then he went on to Redmond. I remember Padraig O'Donnallan [a cousin of her father's, and a noted Irish scholar], and he was visiting our house, and himself and my father were talking, and I was listening to them.

'My father was saying, "Padraig, what do you think of this new leader we have, Willie Redmond – John Redmond's son?"

'"Arrah, Willie," he said, "forget them. Forget the Parnellites. They're dead. There's a new party coming up now," he said. "It's called Sinn Fein."

'My mother had no Irish, you know. She was from Headford. And she said, "What kind of a name is that?"

'And Padraig said, "It means *Ourselves*." Because we were to rely on ourselves from now on, and not be relying on the foreigner." That now would be away back in 1912.

'Now just a week before Easter Week 1916, there were two young people, brother and sister, trying to go to America. They were our next-door neighbours, nearly. And we were fond of them and we'd like them to get on. And the daughter, Brigid, was younger than the son. And they were waiting until Brigid would become eighteen, and Bartley, her brother, twenty-one or twenty-two at this time. He had gone up to the consulate several times to get a passport to go to America, but he couldn't get going. And they were teaching him at home: he never went to school. So, just the week before Easter word came that the lad had got the visa to go to America, and the rejoicing was all over the village.

'So everybody got ready and they were to have an American Wake, the night before they went to America. And everybody brought something to the wake, do you see? My mother and father went to the wake, and that was a few days before Good Friday and they were to sail on Easter Monday. So they left on Easter Saturday and we all went up to the station to see them off. And such crying as there was, because in those days, you never expected to come back again. I was only a child and I couldn't understand these two things: they were all so joyous before, and why are they all crying today, now they're going? The mother was shaking hands with everybody a few days before and saying how delighted she was that Bartley was going to America, and here she was on the station at Oughterard and she throwing her arms around him and kissing him and hugging him and there was all this weeping.

'Then I heard the train coming in on the cutting edge from Clifden – it would make a noise going through a tunnel – and then the crying and the weeping – everyone was crying. And they went down to their carriage and got in. (Either to Cobh or to Galway. It might be into Galway they went. The Hamburg-Amerika used to sail from Galway in those days.) So they were gone. And a week passed – and they were back again! What happened? Every ship was brought to a standstill – no ship was allowed out. There was an insurrection in Dublin. And that's how I learned about Easter 1916.

'They didn't go for fifteen months after that (to America). And when they went, nobody knew they were gone! They didn't create any commotion. She came over afterwards, Brigid, she came back to visit. But Bartley never came back.

'As for the insurrection – first, we thought it was a terrible thing, but when they were all executed, that's when all our minds were changed.'

One Black Day

Nancy Flynn-McFadden

'AND YOUR HAIR looks good and strong, so I don't expect you to lose it, but I'll put you in touch with a hairdresser, and she will come in and let you try on some wigs.'

She sat in her hospital bed numbed by the devastating news that the radical mastectomy had not been enough to rid her of the cancer and that she would have to undergo a course of chemotherapy; 'and treatment once a month for four months, after which you will receive treatment twice monthly for a period of six months'.

'No, no, no,' she screamed silently, trying to take in all this awful news without losing her head. Four months and six months, it was an effort to even add after hearing this news. 'My God! That's almost a year,' she whispered to the brash young doctor, who was sitting busily leafing through his notes while his team of student doctors lined the wall looking on helplessly.

'I must be dying,' she thought to herself, afraid to voice her thoughts for fear it would prove it true.

'Now,' the young doctor said, 'there are leaflets with information on chemotherapy and how best to manage it, which you must read.'

At last she found courage and said vehemently, 'I will not read them!'

'But you must,' insisted this healthy young male, annoyance edging into his voice.

She persisted in her refusal, 'No, I'm not ready yet,' all the time thinking, 'How dare you expect me to accept all this within minutes of hearing this awful news?'

'I wish they would all leave me in peace.' They did. Quietly they left, one by one, some with wan smiles on their faces, others trying to avoid eye contact with her. She almost felt sorry for them having to witness the breaking of this dreadful news, day in, day out.

Now that she was alone in the silence of her room, she felt she was suffocating. 'I must get out of here immediately,' she thought. But, even the act of getting out of bed took some manoeuvring, so, slowly and carefully, she made her way to the wardrobe and opened the door. 'Oh Lord! Nothing there, no clothes, no shoes, no bag. I'm trapped, this is my prison.' She looked towards the window, only to realise she was on the third floor.

'Trapped. Trapped,' she kept repeating with tears streaming down her face and blind panic choking her. She slowly climbed back into bed trying desperately to shut out the memory of the last thirty minutes and the death sentence they brought.

'My God! What will my husband and children do? What will my parents and my brother do? How do I tell them? How will they cope? I waited so long for my children and now I'll never see them grow up.' In minutes she was zooming years ahead, worrying about the future when she herself thought she had none.

Then a knock on the door, and two ladies she barely knew came in to visit – the last two people on earth she needed to see at that moment. She tried to act normal and make small talk, but it was almost impossible while her news was doing laps around her head. 'Will they know by looking at me?' she wondered. 'I wish they would go, please God make them go soon.' And they did. And the silence was even worse than making small talk. More visitors. More small talk. By now, totally panic stricken, she felt like screaming, but she managed to control the urge and eventually those visitors left.

'I must call home with the news. But what do I say? Everyone was so sure we'd got it in time, including the surgeon. How could they all have got it so wrong? God, where are you now? I trusted you and now I need you more than ever – but will you be there for me through this ordeal? Right now I must brace myself, get myself down that corridor to the phone and try to sound confident and in control.'

She felt about 110 years old as she walks to the phone, now noticing everyone she meets along the corridor, scrutinising their faces and wondering what news they received today? 'They all seem so carefree. Lord, I wish I could go back to yesterday, but now a day like yesterday will never dawn for me again. This cloud called chemotherapy will darken my waking moments from now on.'

'Hello,' she tried to say brightly when she heard the coins drop in the box, but no other words would come. After a long pause, she regained her composure and tried to tell in a matter-of-fact voice the latest news. She didn't fool her husband or family as they all played their parts in consoling and soothing her, as if they heard every day from some family member about to undergo this treatment, while they hastily prepared to leave on the long journey to be with her. They knew they were boarding a ship, which would take them on uncharted waters, and they prayed they would all ride the storm, because her pain was their pain and her terror was now theirs also.

Meanwhile back in her ward, she counted the hours until their arrival. She heard a knock on her door, and her heart leapt. 'They couldn't be here already could they?' But no, it was that doctor again, just as bright and breezy as before. He had come to tell her that at that very moment, a lady next door to her was receiving chemotherapy and that he would like her to accompany him now to see how it was administered. She could take no more from him, so she shouted, 'No, no, no, I don't want to see it, I'm not ready. Can't you understand?' He shrugged his shoulders appearing to be mystified at her reaction and said he would come back later. 'No!' she said, 'I don't want to see you again – please send somebody else.'

Alone again, she wept bitterly and wondered how on earth she would react when her family arrived. She would have to be strong for them. 'God, where are you? Padre Pio, are you listening? I can't even pray now. Hail Mary . . . I can't remember the Hail Mary . . . Oh my God, please help me, Mary, you're a mother, surely you'll understand. Help me, please; I think I'm going mad.'

The door opened quietly – they were here, the family had arrived, each one trying to smile convincingly, but they were not fooling her either. But most importantly for her, they were here and she was alone no more.

Sitting, reading her book, six years later, she wondered what had triggered her memory down that dark lane and back to those black days again, and then she noticed the advertisement for wigs. She had lost her hair during the treatment, but now she had a fine head of hair again, just like she had on that awful day the doctor came in.

'Thank you, God: you were listening after all.'

The *Poitín* Priest

Aodhán Ó Céileachair

THE LONG-ENDURING sixteen-mile round trips to the Latin school would be over by June. John was a diligent student and was expected to do well in life, maybe becoming a teacher or a doctor, or getting a good position in the Civil Service. However, this young country lad had felt the calling to serve God for some time. He would probably have been influenced by his friend, Michael, from down the valley and by Frank, from the adjoining hill, who were now third- and fifth-year students in Maynooth.

John knew that Michael's and Frank's parents could afford to send the lads to the seminary, but what of his own family circumstances? Michael's people had good arable land, and every year they set twelve acres of potatoes, which were then sold in the local town. Frank's parents were blessed with having a good strip of bog over in Aughagréine. You could get surely twenty spit of turf out of each bog hole. Every year they covered the hollow bank and cutaway with the best of black turf, which was then sold on to the local hospital. With good financial management, these two families were comfortably putting their sons through school.

John Tom and Maggie Devine couldn't see themselves getting much of a return from setting potatoes down in the rushy bottoms. They couldn't sacrifice one generation on behalf of another by exploiting their small parcel of bog for commercial purposes. They also had two daughters coming of age when dowries would be needed to assure them of a future. Maggie thought to herself that maybe they should have let their eldest daughter, Annie, go to train for nursing in Maidstone instead of offering her the £200 the night before she departed. Well, that was in the past, and sure didn't it set her and her husband up; he started a bit of calf dealing with the money. Trying to cope with all of this on twelve acres with four cows, a bullock and a horse that was borrowed wouldn't be easy. John Tom's brother in America would help out, but he couldn't be expected to foot the whole bill. Maynooth would be a costly place.

The couple sat by the open-hearth fire and pondered on how they could send John to the clerical college. John Tom knew that there would be a good return from making *poitín*, and he was an experienced hand at the still from his younger days. But it was only two years ago, after a rumpus at a wake, that Canon Boyle denounced from the altar the making or drinking of *poitín* and referred to it as the Devil's Brew. After much discussion, the pair decided to play the devil at his own game. What would be wrong with it? 'Didn't Our Lord change spring water into wine at the wedding feast of Cana, and surely his cause wasn't as noble as ours.' Hell or high water couldn't be allowed stand in John's way of honouring his commitment to God.

Soon the word went round that the Devines were gone a bit odd after they erected a six feet high thorny wire fence all around the house. This talk of oddness suited the family down to the ground. What was once a good *céilí* house soon became a fortress. No one was admitted to their dwelling except the near neighbours, including myself. We were sworn to secrecy. John Tom bought a shining new still from Big Pat Lawrence, a tinker who was camped on the Bog Road. They were now in business and busy distilling. Dipping my finger into the first run just to get the taste was a real treat for a twelve-year-old like me who had heard all the great stories about the power of *poitín*.

Every night a steady stream of people could be heard walking down the half-closed-in lane by the Lough. They came from far and near for bottles of the brew, as it had the reputation of being the purest in the area. John Tom and Maggie convinced themselves that it was only used for cattle cures and didn't break the canon's code.

John, as expected, did well in his exams and was ordained in Maynooth after seven years. His parents were proud people when he celebrated his first mass in the local church. The Devines were soon cured of their oddness, and their home reverted to being an ordinary *céilí* house again.

Fr John went off to the missions and was known for ever as the *poitín* priest. The fact that he was schooled on the proceeds of the illicit brew never hampered him one bit in spreading the Gospel in several continents.

Follow Your Dream

Brendan Power

WE IRISH HAVE long had a love affair with horses and horse racing, so it was no surprise that when the Muldoons and the McEvoys made their separate ways across the Irish Sea the love of the turf travelled with them. In later years, when Tom Muldoon met and married Leah McEvoy in their adopted home of Manchester, that love of horses was destined to become an integral part of the family.

Little Joe, their youngest son, had never seen a horse race, so, for him, the household conversations about bloodstock and betting meant nothing until one fateful day in 1926. It was a time some called the Roaring Twenties, and others knew as the depression. It was mid-way between two world wars, and just twelve months since the general strike, but Joe was not thinking of that. His mind was fixed firmly on a photo in the newspaper lying on the kitchen table.

It was a photo of the 1926 Grand National winner Jack Horner, and standing beside the horse was the winning jockey, Billy Watkinson, surrounded by all kinds of luminaries. Joe noticed something unusual about the picture; like him, Billy Watkinson was small, smaller than those around him, but the unusual thing was that Billy was not being teased or being bullied. In fact, he was the centre of attention; he was the one they were all looking up to. On that day Joe discovered that being small could sometimes be an advantage; on that day he determined that he, too, would experience the thrill of crossing that winning line; and on that day his dream was born.

It was a big dream for a little boy, and an even bigger dream for the son of an Irish immigrant from the back streets of 1920s Manchester. Boys from that area worked in factories, or on the docks, or in coalmines. But not this boy. He was determined to do whatever it took to turn his dream into reality even though he had yet to see his first race. He developed a voracious appetite for reading; he read books, magazines, newspapers, in fact he read everything he could find about jockeys and about racing.

And then, proving once again that if you make room for it, it will come, an amazing thing happened. Joe was eating fish and chips from the local chip shop, and as always in those days, they were wrapped in newspaper. When the chips were finished, the newspaper remained, and his appetite for food was replaced by his appetite for reading. As he looked down at the paper, he could hardly believe his eyes. It was the tiniest of advertisements, but to him it stood out like a giant billboard: 'Stable boys and apprentice jockeys wanted.' He wrote a letter, he got an interview, he told them about his dream, demonstrated the knowledge he had gained from reading, and then went home to wait.

Now, at last, a month later, the postman had brought the letter, the first time Joe had ever seen a letter addressed to himself. He held it tightly in his hands, he could hardly steady himself enough to open it, his whole body was shaking with anticipation, and then, with the family gathered around, he slowly opened it.

He read it, he passed it around, he could not believe it. 'I've got the job . . . I've got the job!' His shouts could be heard in the next house, probably even in the next street, tears rolled down his cheeks, and a ray of sunshine brightened that rainy day. His dream was unfolding, the job was his, but it was in a place he had never heard of – Chantilly. It was in France. France! He had never even been outside Manchester before; remember this was the 1920s. But if the job was in France, then France was where he was going.

Two hundred and fifty miles of bumpy roads in an unheated bus, and then across London to catch the boat train to Dover was just the start. When *The Maid of Kent* docked in Calais over twenty-four hours after he left Manchester, fourteen-year-old Joe was not just in another country; he felt like he was in another world. All around him people were talking, but he could not understand a word. He looked at the words his mother had written down for him and matched them to the signs around him to find the train. A long wait, another of the day-old sandwiches from Manchester, and he was on his way again, this time to his dream and the place he had first heard of just a few weeks ago, Chantilly.

It was then that Joe discovered dreams can sometimes become nightmares. The stables were not exactly what he had expected or hoped for. His accommodation was little better than the horses', and at 6 a.m. the next morning he started work, cleaning out the stables. The work was hard and there was no one to talk to; they all spoke a different language. Some nights he would cry himself to sleep and wonder why he was there. But every day as he stood and watched the jockeys take the horses out for their morning run, his dream was rekindled. He looked again at the crumpled newspaper photo of Billy Watkinson and remembered why he was there.

Gradually he learnt to speak French, and as soon as he could communicate, life looked brighter. He made friends with some of the jockeys; his appetite for knowledge returned, and his dream of crossing that winning line took on a new lease of life.

It was three long years before he moved on from stable duties to apprentice jockey, and the first time he put on his helmet and rode out of the yard, he felt 10ft tall. Racing was still a long way away, however, and Joe worked hard at learning the skills he would need on the racecourse. He travelled all over France, sharing the transporter with the horses, helping the jockeys and dreaming of the day his turn would come.

He rode in minor events around the country, but it was to be five more years before Joe finally achieved his dream. In the 1936 Grand Prix de Bordeaux, the hardship, the work, the deprivation and the loneliness faded from his mind as he crossed the winning line on Eucalyptus with his hand held high and a fading newspaper cutting under the saddle.

It Only Takes a Second

Maureen O'Halloran

STEVE WAS AS fit as the proverbial fiddle. He was a non-smoker, he trained regularly, played rugby and spent much of his time building our dream home in the country, which we moved in to just two weeks after his fortieth birthday. He lived for his family, and we had no reason to believe he was in anything but the best of health.

As his wife I knew him better than most. We were so close that half the time we even knew what each other was thinking, and I felt like the luckiest woman alive. There was one thing I could never understand, however: why did I always worry about his heart? Heart trouble is reserved for smokers, or older people, or the overweight, or anyone except a forty-year-old rugby player – isn't it? For years I had tried to put my worries to the back of my mind, but they kept cropping up for no apparent reason. It bothered me, but seemed so silly that I never mentioned it to Steve; it must have been the only thing I ever kept secret from him.

Just a month after moving into the new house, I had the strangest feeling that I was suddenly alone; the feeling of loss was so painful that I believed Steve had died. I was out walking with a friend, and when she saw the look on my face she asked what was wrong, but, although I heard her, the voice seemed to come from far away. Eventually I snapped out of it, but for a while it scared the hell out of me.

The next night was my birthday, and Steve and I went out with a few friends. We had a great night, the best in a long time, and I remember telling Steve how much I loved him. A couple of days later we decided to take the children to Galway for the day as a treat. During dinner I noticed that Steve did not look so well; he was burping a lot but just passed it off as a gastric tummy. The burping got worse and a sickly feeling came over me. My mind immediately went back to those thoughts I had on my walk a few days earlier. Steve suggested we go home as he wasn't feeling the best, so we headed for the car.

He was feeling dizzy at this stage. I was feeling very scared, and although he protested that it wasn't necessary, I headed for the hospital to get him checked over. Within five minutes of our arrival at the hospital, Steve was fighting for his life. The doctors couldn't understand what was happening, but his heart was doing over 300 beats per minute and he was fading fast. Standing in the resuscitation room watching everything going on, I was in shock; I couldn't believe this was happening. It was like something out of a television programme. I was staring at my husband who was not moving. Needles were going in everywhere, but nothing was making any difference. He looked at me, and at that point I knew he was going. He was just about able to say 'My wife', and that was it. A nurse took me out and I could hear the doctor shouting, 'Cardiac arrest, everyone stand clear.' The electric shock treatment worked and they got a steady rhythm.

Later that night they explained that Steve had WPW syndrome, the rare type that was always fatal. It was a miracle that he had survived long enough to get to hospital. He was transferred to St James' Hospital in Dublin for an emergency operation, where the specialist told us that he had never known anyone with WPW as bad as Steve to have survived. The readings he got from Steve's heart were unbelievable.

They got rid of the seven extra pathways in Steve's heart, but six months later Steve had another attack, and that's when it was discovered that Steve had two more pathways. They were inoperable as they were at the top part of the heart, so he was put on medication and went on to have another two attacks. Steve and I know that there is a chance that he will have other attacks, but hopefully the medication will do the trick, and if not, we will just have to find something else that will work.

If it's possible, I think I love him even more today than I did all those years ago when we first met, and now we know why we were meant to be together: God wanted it that way. While he was recovering in hospital, Steve said, 'Thank God you didn't listen to me and bring me home or I would be gone.'

My answer was, 'I haven't listened to you since we got married and I wasn't about to start today!' We still laugh about that, and the fact that we can still laugh is a blessing.

We are planning for a long life, but we treat every day as something special. After all, not many people get a second chance. Your life may not be as traumatic – neither was ours before that day in Galway – but no matter what is going on in your life, never forget to tell that someone special that you love them every single day of your life. It is so important and it only takes a second.

A Spider and a King

Ranald Macdonald

We all know the story of Robert the Bruce, king of Scotland, and the humble spider that taught him never to give up. But very few people know that the events of the story took place in Ireland, and that the spider itself was Irish. For Robert had suffered great setbacks in the battle against the English and fled across the North Channel to wind-swept Rathlin Island, off County Antrim. He slumped down in a cave there, in the fall of the year, and tasted the bitterness of defeat. Suddenly he saw a spider – a native of this land – spinning its web. The king watched in fascination. He understood that he must also not give up, but must try and try again. In time he set sail for Scotland once more and fought his greatest battle, Bannockburn, keeping in his heart the great truth he learned from the little spider in the cave in Ireland.

But what did the spider see? That is soon told . . .

The golden grass is tarnished now, and the red leaves are dashing in the wind. But I have been secure in my cave for a number of days. There are a few small flies that come in from the wet wind to seek shelter. I will end my days eating them. And when the nights grow cold I will be content to turn as grey and quiet as the walls of this cave. A spider needs no eternity, just enough hours to spin his web and dine.

But who is this? A flash of flaring torchlight – do they want to blind me with their flames? The clang of weapons dropped to the ground. Shields, swords, spears – I know these types. They are soldiers, tired of war. They have come to drop their defeat on the floor of my cave. A spider is at his most dangerous when he is still. And if you break my web, do you think I will cease to fight?

Wet leather – it leaves a pungent smell. But look at them! They flop to the floor. There is blood, I can tell. Will they die here?

That one is the man they follow, the king I should say. A foreign king, by the looks of him. What does he want here in Ireland? His helmet has a crown, flashing in the firelight. I could spin my web on those points. Look at him – he's running scared, he's hiding from himself. What better place to do it in, than in a cave?

Oh, he's coming here! Look at those stiff joints. He can hardly lower himself to the ground. Well, king, are you comfortable? Wrap yourself in your cloak. It's rich and red and safe from prying eyes.

Now I have work to do. It is the time of the long threads. I have three edges of rock to catch and then a leap into the middle. A foothold on the left will start me off. Past the king's slumped head. The thread I have already spun is fine to see and graceful in the torchlight. I prefer semi-darkness – flies don't see me then. Now over his shoulder and up to the top. He's not asleep. He's thinking he is near the end. I know the signs.

There. It is a long way to that point. An abyss to some. I'm not sure I can make it. But the web depends on linking up the right. I will go. After all, I have enough fight left in me.

Down – down, down! Stop! No – too far! Ah, that means the long climb back.

Did I shout? No. I thought out loud perhaps. But that king there has lifted his head. What does he think he's looking at? Look and learn, oh king – this is how it's done!

Up – up, up! Rapidly, in mid air. I have faith in this strand. Ah-h-h! I've fallen again, away from the line on the side. How will I ever get there? A man can take on too much after all.

I am getting to know the outlines of this cave quite well. The view from halfway up is neither good nor bad. He's still watching. This is what you do if you are serious about life: climb. Admit to yourself there is more to come, but the final goal is in sight.

There. One more drop! Can I reach it? Nearly, nearly – keep going! OH! Which of my eight legs should land first? It doesn't matter. Why, the stone tastes good on this side!

Now my feet are firmly on the ground, the three lines are secure, I can go back to the middle and build.

Are you still looking? You are a king of sorts. You will have to learn your own worth. To the eyes of a spider a man is a small creature – he fails and then forgets himself.

But look – I see this man growing! He is nearly the size of me now. He is equal to his wounded men, to the battle he will face. The firelight shines in his eyes. He sees the victory ahead! Return to your land, oh king! This spider from Ireland salutes you!

. . . So. The cold time is coming. A few more dreams, a few more meals. And then the grey lines of the cave will draw me down into peaceful sleep.

Despite Adversity

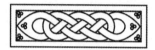

Joe Mullarkey

I GREW UP in east Mayo in the late 1940s and 1950s, attending the local monastery school run by the Franciscan
brothers who tried to educate us by terror, unless you were
a member of one of the few middle-class families, or large
farmers, in the area. Then you might escape the unending
physical punishment.

Growing up through adolescence, the realisation that
many of us would have to emigrate grew as we watched
older school friends taking the boat. We watched as close-
knit families, indeed whole villages, were decimated while
local politicians and church leaders, together with local and
national media, acquiesced and turned a blind eye. The
young people of the country were being exported, many
badly prepared for life in an urban environment without the
family support that had been part of their life at home.

Growing up in Mayo my passion was Gaelic football;
playing at minor and senior level for Ballyhaunis, my last
competitive game in Ireland was for East Mayo seniors
against West Mayo in Westport in 1961. The previous winter I had worked in England but had returned home in early
spring hoping to find work and continue playing football.

Unable to find employment, I returned to Bolton in
Lancashire only to find the cotton industry in decline with
the loss of 10,000 jobs. Returning to the job I had the

previous year was no longer an option, so the next three weeks were spent trying to find employment. Eventually I found work on a farm on the outskirts of Bolton, having to catch the first bus there at 6.30 a.m. every morning. Fortunately, in a matter of a few weeks I found new employment in a factory producing film roll. All the time I was waiting for a place in the Bolton Transport Department training school, following my earlier application for a job as a bus conductor. My intention was that after qualifying as a conductor I would enter the driving training school to obtain a PSV driving licence. The Public Service Vehicle licence would, I hoped, be my passport to a driving job in newly emerging Irish tourism industry.

In Bolton I was able to continue playing Gaelic football with Shannon Rangers, competing in the Lancashire league and championship. Occasionally I also played hurling for them. Working on the buses was, in many respects, very enjoyable, but it had one big drawback; we had to work alternate Sundays, and as all football was played on a Sunday, trying to get the shift finished in time to get to the venue posed difficulties, to say the least. There were times when I had to pay somebody to work my shift and then, at a later date, work his or her shift!

My life changed a couple of years later when I decided to explore the employment market again. Travelling home late from work one night, I took a short cut across a railway line and was hit by a passing train, losing both legs above the knee; only the fitness gained from playing football saved my life. I was just turned twenty-two years of age, an emigrant without much family support. Although I had a brother and sister living in England, both had their own family responsibilities.

After a period of hospitalisation and rehabilitation lasting about eighteen months, I managed to find work with an engineering company, assembling counting instruments. It was here that I became involved in the trade union movement, where a lifetime of involvement and commitment has brought a good deal of satisfaction. As a senior shop steward for over thirty years, I availed of the union's education courses to improve my own education.

Like so many others, I was unprepared for events that flowed from the civil rights campaign that began in Northern Ireland in 1969. The Irish community living in Britain had no community structures that would cope following the 1974 Birmingham and Guilford pub bombings and the introduction of the Prevention of Terrorism Act. Numerous Irish people, like myself, joined left wing British groups in an attempt to oppose the legislation only to find some of those organisations were primarily interested in using Irish issues to attack the establishment.

In the early eighties Irish activists in Britain established the Irish in Britain Representation Group to represent the interests of the community in culture, education, welfare, anti-Irish racism and various political issues of concern. The Bolton branch had a comparatively large membership of over 100 but, as with most organisations, only about 30 per cent were active members. They organised Irish language classes, céilí and set dance classes, the Bolton Irish festival, Irish input into multi-cultural festivals and an Irish radio programme, as well as Irish representation on the Bolton Race Equality Council and the local authority's Ethnic Minorities Joint Consultative Council. I had the honour of representing the community as national vice-president of the Irish in Britain group, branch chairman of the Ethnic Minorities Council and PRO of the Birmingham Six northwest campaign group.

For ten years I chaired the Bolton branch of Comhaltas Ceoltóirí Éireann and was PRO for eight, with another three years as PRO for the northern region, during which I wrote a column in the Irish Post.

Despite all the activities I managed to get married in 1972 and am now the proud grandfather of five wonderful grandchildren. My life has turned full circle, and although I won't be playing football this time, we are now returning to live in Ireland after over forty years in exile.

My purpose in writing this is to reach out to others who, because of an accident or illness, may have their lifestyle disrupted. Don't despair, life will offer you alternatives. If my accident had never happened, I would have returned to live in Ireland and continued to play football. Following the accident I chose to remain in England as it seemed to offer the best chance of getting employment, and as a consequence of that decision I did many things that I believe I would otherwise have missed out on. There is no need to wait for something or someone to push us into a decision; the opportunities are there for all of us. We just have to take the initiative and believe in ourselves.

The Grey Man

Patricia Smyth

THE DAY WAS scorching, and the great slabs of limestone rock burnt through the thin soles of her sandals. Little orchids and pink cranesbills peeped shyly up through the deep crevices in the rocky fields of the island. She picked her way warily across the fields, afraid of tripping or twisting her foot along the stony way. She knew every nook and turn of the way back, and all the little gaps in the stone walls that led from one field into another. She passed a huge tombstone tossed up on a boulder, on which many years ago a stone-mason had carved the name of a Bridget Conneely, Born 1832–Died 1864. It had been abandoned in the fields, too heavy to be moved down to the graveyard. She stepped through the gap whence lay the abandoned tombstone and stopped dead in her tracks.

Across the field, perched up on the top of a wall, sat the figure of a little man. He was no more than three feet tall and wore a grey jerkin over grey leggings, and his face was as grey as his clothes. A grey hat was aslant his head, and his long pointed ears accentuated the long pointed chin. Upon his feet were boots that were turned up at the toes. He sat with his arms around his knees, which were drawn up to his chin. Patricia felt chilled at the sight of him. He turned his head and stared at her so that she could see the whites of his eyes, or at least what should have been the whites of his eyes, because these were as black as coal. Instinctively she knew that this was no mortal being.

Petrified, she stood quite still. Was this the famous leprechaun, the little fellow that you are not supposed to take your eye off in case he would vanish? 'No,' she thought, 'he would be dressed in green and perhaps scarlet with a feather in his hat.' She felt terribly afraid. He moved his head slightly, and she could see his hair wild and unkempt sticking up against the cloudless sky. She thought to speak, and glancing momentarily down to her feet in case she stepped into a deep fissure in the limestone slabs, she took a step towards him, and in a split second he was gone. The space on the top of the wall where he had sat was empty against the blue backdrop of that June sky.

It took her ten minutes to scramble over the rest of the stone walls and through the rocky fields back to the guesthouse. 'Holy St Anthony, is it mad you are entirely?' laughed the woman of the house when Patricia told of her meeting with the apparition. No one believed her; some of the other guests guffawed and asked her if she had been on the *poitín*, while others began to make up fabulous stories of their own. Patricia was too shocked to take offence and said no more. But all that night she listened to the great roar of breakers crashing up the beach and the corncrakes croaking their weird prehistoric call in the deep grasses about the house. No one believed she had seen what she could only describe as a fairy.

Her holiday on the island, which had started with such promise of relaxation, had suddenly taken on a feeling of foreboding and suspense. She was afraid to go about exploring on her own again for fear of meeting with the strange creature. And for the rest of the time she avoided the Atlantic side of the island.

Once she returned home she gradually forgot all about her experience. Swiftly the years passed; she studied, worked and eventually married. Having reared a family of six children, she decided to return to work and secured a position in the National Museum. She loved her job in retail in the fine museum shop, where she would spend many hours polishing the Kilkenny glass and arranging jewellery and beautiful paperweights. Her favourite job of all was unpacking the books on all kinds of subjects, including museum artefacts and local history.

Unpacking a box of newly arrived books one day, she noticed the title of one particular book in the pile; it was called *A Field Guide to Irish Fairies*. It was a quiet day with few people in the shop, so she picked up the book and opened it. The exact page at which she opened it was called *The Grey Man*. There she read with amazement a precise description of the figure that so many years ago she had seen on top of the stone wall on the island. This fairy was described as being prevalent along the western seaboard and was not considered to be very lucky.

As the sun threw long shadows across the hall in which she stood, the rosy hue of the marble pillars deepened in its glow. The dust in the sunbeams sparkled like a thousand fairies floating and rising in the silent hall. And Patricia once again felt the same chill that had enveloped her that day in the limestone field. It was true; she had seen something that belonged to another realm.

I know, because that girl was me.

IN THE WOODS

Gabriel Fitzmaurice

X on a tree trunk
Marks no buried treasure here
Children wonder why

A rotting tree stump
In the middle of the woods
Mushrooms with new life

Where there are nettles
There are dock leaves to heal us
In a spot nearby.

Look Before You . . .

Brian Matthews

NEW ROSS IN County Wexford is my hometown. It was a great place to grow up during the 1940s and '50s. The problems that are being highlighted today for children of that time thankfully passed me by. We enjoyed a comfortable lifestyle provided by my father who worked for the Provincial Bank of Ireland, and such a job at that time had 'status'.

My father was a tall, austere man, a product of his upbringing in a stern Church of Ireland family and Waterford boarding school. Generally, he worked from 9 a.m. to about 3.30 p.m. every day. His pastimes were walking, which he did every day, and his car that was his pride and joy! Once a year, on Christmas Eve, he had a drink; a glass of port was drunk to wish us all a Happy Christmas.

Despite this lack of drinking in our home, there was a drinks cabinet, which housed a set of three crystal decanters, kept in a special locked container and always empty! The star attraction in this cabinet, however, was a very special bottle of Redbreast Irish Whiskey. This bottle was a work of art, crowned with a strong red seal, which added to the mystique.

One thing my friends and I in New Ross had in common with other teenagers around the world was that we had all the answers to the problems of the world. One such problem that arose was the infamous boycott in Fethard-on-Sea in

1957. This was Catholic versus Protestant thinking at its very worst and an event that had a major effect on us. So to our discussion about this event, which was to take place behind the boat club, I took the bottle of Redbreast.

Over the course of the afternoon we drank the entire contents – diluting it with red lemonade. When I realised the bottle was entirely empty, I knew I would have to refill it somehow or face the wrath of my father! Cold tea certainly looked the part, and I did a fantastic resealing job. The bottle was put back in its sacred place and there it remained, with the amendments unnoticed, for many more years.

On Easter Sunday 1967 my father died. By then I was married and living in London. Irish funerals are usually great affairs, and, like me, my family all made it home, including relations I had not seen for many years. They were there to offer sympathy and support to my mother, who was, naturally, very upset.

I suggested we had a few drinks in the traditional manner. The bottle of Redbreast came to my mind, but – the bottle was missing! Not since the Irish Crown Jewels were stolen did such a surprise occur. The sacred bottle was MISSING. STOLEN? we asked. Where was it? Which of the relations could have taken it? A vigorous investigation failed to turn up any clue; it was a complete mystery.

The years have passed, and all the older relations from that time are now dead. No trace or sight of the Redbreast was ever seen. We will never know who took it, and only I know that if it was a special whiskey they were after, they certainly got it!

Donal

Patrick Tansey

IT WAS A glorious summer day in 1972; my wife and I were in Skibbereen, in the middle of the simplest, yet most enjoyable, holiday we've ever had. We had rented a horse-drawn gypsy caravan and were trundling through the quiet countryside, listening to every imaginable sound of nature – sounds that, in our normal busy lives, we had almost forgotten existed. Our horse was called Silver, but take my word for it, he was nothing like the Lone Ranger's steed of the same name. He moved at a maximum rate of twelve miles a day!

Every few miles we would come to a stop outside a house and ask if we could fill the water bucket for Silver. 'Of course, come on in,' would be the standard response from the woman of the house, almost insulted that that was all we had asked for. That's the way it was in Ireland back in 1972; most people had nothing, but they were only too willing to share it.

That evening at about 5 p.m., Silver, for the first time, started to increase his speed. We looked at the map the company had provided and saw that we were close to our first farm pull-in. These were small subsistence farmers appointed by the rental company. They would allow us to park, and Silver to graze, in an enclosed field. They also provided us with bathing facilities and a huge breakfast in the morning.

The income they received from this service was a huge benefit in their annual struggle for survival.

The next morning, washed and fed, we went to collect Silver, ready to harness him for the next part of our journey. Disaster. The field was empty. We raced back to tell the farmer. He, his wife and his little son (who had been our 'waiter' at breakfast) hurried to the enclosure. Sure enough, there was no sign of Silver. Farmer O'Brien checked the great wall of hedge around the field and found a gap. 'He's gone through here!' Just as we followed him through the gap, we spotted the horse minding his own business halfway up the mountainside that backed on to the farmer's land. He was free and obviously had no intention of pulling us ever again, or anyone else for that matter.

Mr O'Brien's face was drained of all colour. It was his responsibility to ensure that the overnight field was secure for the horse. 'The company will stop sending people to us after this,' he said. 'I'd better get their help before we lose sight of the horse'.

'Don't do that. I'll get him for you, Dad.' We looked at the child in amazement as he showed a maturity and understanding way beyond his years. Donal was his name and he was just ten years old, a bright ginger-headed lad. His father's face was torn with anxiety. He knew that every passing moment increased the possibility of Silver cantering away out of sight and into what seemed like oblivion, and that meant the loss of a much needed income. On the other hand, if Donal *could* catch him . . .

'Go on then, son, if you think you can.'

Donal raced back to the house and returned with a three-foot length of rope, which he folded carefully and placed down the back of his trousers. He looked up the mountainside; Silver was still in the same place, but keeping a wary eye on us. We watched breathlessly as Donal set off, circumnavigating the mountain, going out of sight, and then, after what seemed an eternity, appearing above Silver, but out of his line of vision. Inch by inch Donal crept down the mountain, freezing to the ground whenever Silver looked like moving.

Eventually, when he was close enough, he hurled himself at Silver, slipping the rope around his neck. The horse offered little resistance, and Donal led him back to the farmhouse. For many years we would recall Donal's bravery, his ingenuity and his self-confidence.

That was in 1972. Now over thirty years later, Ireland is, for the first time in modern history, a booming economy. I wouldn't mind betting that Donal is playing a part in that success, along with many others with the same attitude. Ordinary people doing extraordinary things.

Ambition, Determination and Education

Con Cluskey

WE WERE JUST two Dublin lads, born in Inchicore with very little to distinguish us from anyone else in the area. Life wasn't easy for any of the families, as wages in those days barely covered expenses. My mother spent her life scrimping and saving to try and make ends meet. Okay, we never starved and we were always reasonably dressed, but we were always aware that there was an upper bracket of people with much more.

My mother always emphasised to us the importance of a good education. She scrimped away and managed to send my sister to boarding school in Swinford in Mayo, where she received an excellent education enabling her to join the Civil Service. Then suddenly, my father died from stomach cancer, breaking my mother's heart, and she now had to find new ways to support us. She took in lodgers, she worked late into the night making hats for Clery's Store in Dublin, and she cooked dinner for teachers in the nearby Oblates School. Anything to raise the money needed to support us at school!

And so ambition and determination was born in us. We did what we thought were normal things, going to O'Connell School all the way across Dublin, learning Irish dancing (I gave up dancing at age eleven when they wanted me to wear a kilt; I wasn't wearing a skirt for anyone!), playing the piano, singing and playing at parties and so on.

Then came the mouth organs at school. This was more fun. Blow, suck, suck, blow. We would listen to harmonica groups like the *Hotcha Trio* on Radio Éireann and thought, 'We could do that.' So we recruited another chap to play the third mouth organ that was needed to form a trio!

My mother supplied the money to buy the expensive mouth organs required for the job. We practised like mad and went to auditions for everything. We did all the charity shows, and then we realised that all we were getting from those charity shows was another charity show. So we went professional and started charging £3 for our services. Big deal! Then, out of the blue, one of the auditions paid off, and we got to play on Hughie Green's *Opportunity Knocks*. We could hardly contain our excitement and had to have a day off school and travel to London for that. What a treat for three Dublin schoolboys.

The American *Ed Sullivan Show* came to Ireland looking for talent to appear on a St Patrick's Day TV special. We were selected to play on that for a princely fee of £15. Wow! We met Fred O'Donovan of the Eamonn Andrews Studios, and he recruited us to feature in a twenty-five-week radio series on Radio Éireann called *Odd Noises*. This was the foundation we needed, as we learned a lot from Fred. We called ourselves *The Harmonichords*, and thanks to *Odd Noises* we became famous all over Ireland. Not bad for three Dublin schoolboys.

In 1962 we were asked to tour Britain with Nina and Frederick, and again we thought, not bad for three Dublin lads. We finished up in Manchester where we were asked to perform, but we needed a bigger act singing and playing guitars and bass, which we had added to our repertoire. Again my mother came to the rescue, and she managed to carry two guitars and a bass, plus her luggage, from Dublin to Manchester on the B & I boat!

Next came a summer season in Arbroath, Scotland, with Johnny Logan's father, Patrick O'Hagan, and Hal Roach, the comedian. While we were there Dick Rowe of Decca Records came to see us and asked us to record for him. We changed our name to The Bachelors and recorded a song called 'Charmaine', which hit the British charts at number five. We thought, not bad for three Dublin lads.

Two years later we hit the number one spot in the charts with a song called 'Diane' and became the first Irish group to do so. As The Bachelors we became the first 'Irish boy band' to become a household name worldwide. We spent the next forty years travelling the world entertaining people of all classes and colours. We have mixed with all sorts of people, including royalty, and have had no problems because of our good Irish education paid for by my mother.

Royal Command Performances followed, as did numerous tours and many a TV series. We had the pleasure of inviting my mum to our first Royal Command Performance in 1964 where she finished up in the company of Sammy Davis Junior, Jerry Lewis, and Morecambe and Wise, amongst others.

We are thankful for the great life we've had, and today we enjoy putting something back through our involvement in various charities. Dec became King Rat of the Grand Order of Water Rats, whilst I became president of Elland Rotary Club in Yorkshire, where I live today. We play in many charity golf tournaments and visit Ireland a lot in so doing. I keep my house in Dublin and encourage young people to follow in my footsteps through the Young Enterprise scheme, whilst Dec encourages budding musicians through his website (www.MakeHits.com).

Not bad for two Dublin lads who started out with nothing but talent, ambition, determination and a good Irish education. Unfortunately my mother died in 1978 whilst we were appearing at the ABC Theatre in Blackpool. We brought her back to Dublin to her home, and her body now rests in Glasnevin, but her spirit is always with us. Thanks, Mum.

The Catwoman of Castlequarter

Angela Doyle

THE SIMCOX HOUSEHOLD at Castlequarter, Ballinlough, could not be described as an average one. This charming country cottage, outbuildings and adjoining gardens are home to – at the last count – two adults, two children, forty-five cats (including three three-legged ones), five dogs, three donkeys (including Daisy, aged forty), two pigs, eleven goats, twenty ducks, two hens, two goldfish, tropical fish, one rabbit and one guinea pig.

Janice Simcox, along with her husband, Peter, and two children, Rosie and James, has been running a cat sanctuary from her home since they arrived in Ireland from England in 1995.

Queen of the cat family at Simcox's is Talullah, an aristocratic, pedigree silver chinchilla. She lives indoors, along with some other lucky felines – there are four in the bathroom – but most are accommodated in various ways at the rear of the house. Missy, a yappy Yorkshire terrier-French poodle cross, patrols the yard. The ducks wander freely from place to place, and the goats, in the outbuildings, are keen to put their front legs over the half-doors and lean out, just like old women gossiping over a fence.

Each cat has a name: there's Sexy Ted, Finbarr, Bubbles and Peter, for example. Each cat also has a place in this extraordinary family. There is one one-eyed cat and one deaf feline. Some have personality problems. Some are almost feral. One sick little cat has suspected feline leukaemia. Janice knows the health status and personality quirks of each and every one.

Janice worked for herself in England, providing services to the elderly such as shopping and gardening. 'This is something I always thought I would never be able to do because you have to be a millionaire to buy a house with enough land in England,' she said.

'I met Peter and he didn't laugh at me. "Why shouldn't you chase your dream?" he said.' Then her sister showed her a video taken by a friend who had bought a property in Ireland, a house with rambling gardens, for just £17,000. 'We couldn't believe it, so we ended up buying a house on the telephone,' she said.

They had already sold their house in England when the sale on the house they wanted to buy fell through, so they ended up buying another very quickly. It was only when they arrived in the Castlerea area in 1995 that they realised the house didn't have piped water . . . or doors and windows.

'We had a list of twenty things that we wanted, like a view, mature trees and a location off the road. We never mentioned water, electricity, windows and doors to the auctioneer,' Peter quipped.

They arrived one cold November afternoon with two very young children and a removal van. Janice had to borrow enough from the removal men to get a B&B for the night. The removal men couldn't get the truck near to the house, so they just unloaded all the family's belongings into the field. It was not the perfect start to their new life in Ireland.

The Simcox family stayed and struggled. Peter works nights to earn a living to keep his family and all the animals; he also builds the accommodation for the cats in his spare time. Janice promised him that if he built outdoor homes for the animals, the cats would leave the house. Peter obliged, but there are still several cats living in the cottage.

Janice receives very little funding for her animal sanctuary, and what there is doesn't cover the cost of housing and feeding the animals but does cover vet's fees for vaccination and neutering.

'It's difficult, but we have to keep going. If we don't, what will happen to the cats? I look at them, and I know I can't give up,' Janice said.

Daisy, the forty-year-old donkey, is very much the mascot of the family. She was the first rescue donkey they got, and they had to swap a four-poster brass bed for her. 'The only posh thing we had was the bed, but look at our Daisy now,' she said. 'Before we came to Ireland, we filled boxes with beautiful things for our new home and we had lovely furniture. We had to have car boot sales in Castlerea, and we sold all our nice possessions to buy the basics to keep the animals going. We've got nothing that we saved for.'

She doesn't give animals to people looking for pets as a matter of course. 'I can have a cat here for two or three years before they get a home,' she explained. 'I do not let my cats go to just anyone. I'm not grateful if a farmer comes and says he'll take a couple. No one gets my cats unless I know they're going to be looked after properly.' Cruelty to animals is an issue that Janice feels particularly strongly about.

She does try to convince people that the best way to solve the stray cat problem and also to avoid being unnecessarily cruel is to have cats neutered and vaccinated. It's not expensive, and it eliminates the problem of litters and litters of kittens for which there are no homes.

When cats are cruelly treated, Janice takes it very personally. 'It tears me up inside, and all I feel is anger at people. I feel so strongly about it. People have to have a conscience: they all go to church and these are all God's creatures,' she said.

'I feel as though this is what I was meant to do, but I have to say I would be far happier if there weren't as many stray cats and if people started to take responsibility for their own cats and dogs,' she continued.

Keeping Talullah company in the house is a one-eyed tortoiseshell cat, along with a fluffy, playful ten-week-old kitten known as the Little Black Monster. At the rear of the house, the cats are accommodated in spacious wire pens, some alone and some with company. Peter built the pens and each includes a little house, a paved floor and a tree trunk set in concrete for use as a scratching post and perch. Janice explained that she goes around all the pens at night and gives each group a hot water bottle to keep them warm and contented.

One enclosed building is home to a number of sociable cats. It's heated and there's a radio on at low volume to simulate a homely atmosphere. Think residential playschool, because this is the nearest thing to a feline summer camp there is. The walls are brightly painted, and the room is furnished with all manner of baskets, chairs and tiered bunk beds made from an old shop shelf unit. There are toys, mats, scratching posts and all the necessary paraphernalia to ensure the cats are happy. It's cat heaven.

Finbarr and another three-legged cat are curious and keen to get acquainted. There are approximately fifteen to twenty cats in the room. Janice names them all and explains whether or not they're suitable for rehousing.

Sexy Ted is in the corner. Where did the name come from? Janice explained: 'I just think he's the most gorgeous cat I've ever seen. When I die, I want to come back as a cat and meet Sexy Ted.' He is a beautiful animal, so black as to appear almost blue and with amazingly sensitive eyes, for a cat! All the cats appear to be happy with their home, whether it's temporary or permanent. There's a chorus of purring in the air, despite the busy yapping of the crossbred dog in the adjoining yard.

The pigs are snuffling and rooting in their enclosed area further down the garden, and the ducks are taking a constitutional. While the sanctuary might be a long way off the beaten track – somewhere between Granlahan and Cloonfad – one thing is for sure: no cat could possibly be bored in Castlequarter.

Janice Simcox not only chased her dream but also found someone who was willing to share it. Together, she and Peter are still living that dream in a quiet corner of County Roscommon. The real beneficiaries are the hundreds of unfortunate cats and kittens who have found a place to rest in her sanctuary, and in her heart.

Does He Take Sugar?

Gerry Adams MP

TOM MACAULEY, YOUNGEST son of Martha and Joe MacAuley, was nineteen years old. Joe worked in the office of a Derry shirt factory and he, Martha and Tom lived not far from the Strand Road.

Tom, who had Down's syndrome, had been born ten years after his four brothers and three sisters, and when they had all left home to get married or to seek work abroad, Tom had remained to become the centre of his parents' lives. Already in her late forties when Tom had been born, Martha's health was starting to fail by the time he had reached his teens. But when he wasn't at school Tom rarely left his mother's side.

'Poor Mrs MacAuley,' the neighbours would say when she and young Tom passed by. 'She never gets a minute to herself. That young Tom is a handful, God look to him. Morning, noon and night he's always with his mother. She never gets a break.'

Tom attended a special school and when he was sixteen, the year his father retired from the shirt factory, he graduated to a special project at a day centre on Northland Road. A bus collected him each morning at the corner and brought him back each evening. His father escorted him to the bus and was there again in the evening faithfully awaiting his return.

Tom loved the day centre. He called it work, and it was work of a sort; each week he was paid £3.52 for framing pictures. He also had many new friends and was constantly falling in and out of love with a number of girls who worked with him. Geraldine was his special favourite, but he was forced to admire her from afar; she never gave any indication that she was even aware of his existence. His relationships with the others never really flourished, but at least with them he wasn't as invisible as he was with Geraldine. He could enjoy their company, and one of them, Margaret Begley, wasn't a bit backward about letting him know that she had a crush on him. Tom gave her no encouragement: his heart was with Geraldine. Anyway, he was too shy for Margaret's extrovert ways.

Tom's parents knew nothing of all his feelings towards the girls, but they knew that the work was good for him. At times he would return home excited or annoyed by something which had occurred at the day centre, and when this happened Martha knew the instant she saw him. When he was excited, perhaps from having had a trip to the pictures or when his supervisor praised his work in front of everyone, he radiated happiness. When he was annoyed, he stammered furiously.

On these occasions he rarely volunteered information, and Martha and Joe soon learned that it was useless to question him. Under interrogation he would remain stubbornly non-committal, and if pressed he became resentful and agitated. Left to his own devices, though, he would reveal, in his own time, usually by his own series of questions, the source of his discontent. Tom's questions followed a pattern.

'MMMM Ma,' he would say, 'DDD Does Mick Mick Mickey BBBBradley know how how how to dddddrive a cacaacar?'

'No, son, Mickey wouldn't be allowed to drive a car.'

'Hhhhehe says he cacacan.'

'He's keeping you going, Tom.'

'If we had a cacacar could I drdrdrive it?'

'Of course,' Martha would smile. 'Your daddy would teach you.'

'Right,' Tom would say, and that would be that.

Work gave Tom a small but important measure of independence, and his experiences at work rarely impinged on his home life. Martha and Joe's relationship with him remained largely as it had been before. They still never permitted him to go off alone, except in his own street. Tom didn't seem to mind. He collected postcards. When he was at home he spent most of his time counting and recounting, sorting and resorting his collection in scrapbooks and old shoeboxes and writing down their serial numbers in jotters which his father bought him.

He also did small chores around the house. It was his job to keep the coal-bucket filled, and he always cleared the table after dinner. Occasionally he helped with the dishes, and he fetched dusters and polish or things like that for his mother when she did her cleaning. Most mornings he also collected the paper in the corner shop while his mother prepared the breakfast. Seamus Hughes, the shopkeeper, always delighted him with his greeting.

'Ah, Tom, you'll be wanting to catch up on the news. Here's your paper.'

Tom would be especially happy if there was anyone else in the shop to hear Seamus's remarks. He would beam with pleasure and mumble his red-faced and affirmative response.

His father and he went for walks regularly every Saturday and Sunday afternoon, and Tom loved these outings. His usual facial expression was blandly benign, but when he smiled he smiled with his whole face, and during the walks with his father the smile rarely left him. Everyone knew the pair and had a friendly greeting for them both. Usually they walked out the line where the doggymen exercised their greyhounds, and on one memorable Sunday they took the back road across the border and went the whole way as far as Doherty's Fort at the

Grianán of Aileach in Donegal. The following day was the only occasion on which Tom missed work; he was so tired after their outing that Martha couldn't rouse him from the bed. His father joked with him about it afterwards.

At Christmas there was a pantomime at Tom's work. Tom had a small part as Aladdin's servant. All the parents and families along with various agencies and local dignatories were invited to the centre for an open night. Samples of handicrafts were on display and photographs of their projects adorned the walls. On the night of the performance when the audience were milling around in the main corridor sipping tea and lemonade while they waited for the show to start in the main hall, one of Tom's workmates, a young man from the Brandywell called Hughie, suddenly started yelling and bawling.

At first everyone just looked away and pretended that nothing was amiss, but as Hughie's parents failed to pacify him the commotion increased. One of the supervisors intervened, but that only seemed to make Hughie worse. Apparently this was the first year that Hughie had not had a part in the pantomime. When rehearsals had begun earlier in the year, he had insisted that he didn't want a part. Now when he saw the gathering and the excitement of his friends as they prepared for the evening's performance and when it was too late for him to do anything, he had changed his mind. He wanted to be in the pantomime and nothing would satisfy him except that.

His parents were distracted, and as Hughie continued his bad-tempered hysterics, their consternation spread to the audience. Some of the pantomime players came from the big hall, where they were nervously finalising last-minute arrangements, to see what the racket was about. Tom was among them, dressed in an oriental-type outfit made by his mother from old curtains and an old dressing-gown.

No one paid much attention when Tom left his costumed

friends and made his way through the throng to where Hughie stood bawling in the corner, surrounded by his distraught parents and two of the day centre supervisors. Then to everyone's surprise Tom intervened.

'Ex-cuse me,' he said to Hughie's parents, and without waiting for a reply he pushed his way past them before stopping with his face close to Hughie's.

'Shughie, ddddddon't be be ge ge gett-ing on like th th this,' he stammered.

Hughie ignored him. Tom looked at his friend beseechingly. Hughie still ignored him and carried on bawling.

Tom leaned over and whispered in Hughie's ear, then stopped and looked at him again. Hughie continued to bawl but less stridently now. Tom leaned over and whispered again in his ear. Hughie stopped. Tom looked at him once more.

'All rrrright?' he asked.

Hughie nodded.

Tom turned and walked back to his friends. As they watched him, Martha and Joe were as pleased as Punch, especially when Tom's supervisor came over and shook their hands.

'That's a great lad you have there. He's a credit to the two of you the way he handled Hughie.'

After the pantomime Hughie's father was equally lavish in his praise.

'I'm really grateful for the way your Tom quietened down our Hughie. It's wonderful the way they can communicate with each other in a way that the rest of us can't. Your Tom's the proof of that. The way he was able to get through to our Hughie. None of the rest of us could do that. It never fails to amaze me. Tom's a great lad.'

On the way home that night Joe asked Tom what he had said to Hughie. Tom was pleased with all the attention he was receiving, but he was non-committal about his conversation with Hughie. When Joe pressed the issue Tom got a little edgy. Martha squeezed Joe's arm authoritatively.

'Leave things as they are,' she whispered.

Joe nudged Tom.

'I'm not allowed to ask you anything else!' he joked.

Tom smiled at him.

'That's good,' he said.

Over the Christmas holidays all Tom's brothers and sisters visited home. Tom especially enjoyed his nephews and nieces and the way they brought the house alive with their shouting and laughing, crying and fighting.

A few days after Christmas, Martha's sister Crissie came to visit them as she always did. During her visits Tom spent a lot of time in his room sorting his postcards. He was in the living room when Aunt Crissie arrived – his mother insisted on that – but after the flurry of greetings had subsided Tom made his escape. A retired schoolteacher and a spinster, the oldest of Martha's sisters, Aunt Crissie tended to fuss around him, and this made him uneasy. Joe shared his son's unease in the presence of Aunt Crissie, thinking her a busybody but all the same marvelling at her energy and clearness of mind.

'I hope I'm as sprightly as that when I get to her age,' he would say to whoever was listening.

Crissie hugged Tom and held him at arms' length for a full inspection. 'Tommy's looking great, Martha,' she said.

She always called Tom Tommy. He shifted from foot to foot and gave her his best grin.

'Thhhh tank th thank thank you, Aunt CiciciCrisssssie.'

'I've-brought-you-a-little-something-for-your-stocking, Tommy.'

When Aunt Crissie spoke to Tom directly she did so very slowly. She also raised her voice a little. She always brought him two pairs of socks.

'Thhhh tank th thank thank you, Aunt CiciciCrisssssie.'

'Away you go now, Tom,' his mother said.

Tom and his father usually went off together for a while before their dinner, the highlight of Aunt Crissie's visit. By that time Crissie and Martha were in full flow on a year of family gossip. This continued through the dinner of tasty Christmas Day leftovers until, appetite and curiosity satisfied, Aunt Crissie turned her attention again to Tom. She had poured the tea and was handing around the milk and sugar.

'Does he take sugar?' she asked Joe.

'Do you, Tom?' Joe redirected the question to his son.

'Nnno, Da,' Tom replied in surprise.

Martha looked sharply at her husband. Aunt Crissie saw the glance and apologised quickly.

'I'm-sorry, Tommy. Of-course-you-don't. I-remember-now. Your-mother-tells-me-you're-getting-on-very-well-at-the-day-centre.'

'Aaayye, I am.'

Joe intervened. He was anxious to smooth things over.

'Tom was in the pantomime. It was a great night. They've a great team of people involved with that centre. And all the kids love it. Tom really likes it down there. And he has plenty of friends.'

'It must be very rewarding work for the people involved,' Crissie suggested. She, too, was anxious that the awkwardness be forgotten.

'Tom's supervisor says she wouldn't work with any other kids,' Martha said. 'We were talking to her after the pantomime, and she said that Down's syndrome cases are the easiest to work with.'

'They retain the innocence and trust that the rest of us lose,' said Joe, 'and you know something, they are well able to communicate with one another in a way the rest of us will probably never understand. Isn't that right, Tom?'

Tom looked up from his tea and smiled blankly at his father.

'Wait till you hear this, Crissie,' Joe continued. 'Before the pantomime another lad, Hughie, a friend of Tom's, threw a tantrum, and the only one who could calm him down was Tom. It just goes to show you. Nobody else could get through to him; then Tom spoke quietly to him, and the next thing Hughie was as right as rain. Isn't that right, Martha?'

Martha took up the story from there and recounted the pantomime night episode. When she was finished Aunt Crissie turned to Tom.

'Well done, young man. It's wonderful that you were able to do that. What did you say, by the way?'

Joe chuckled.

'That's something we'll never know. Eh, Tom?'

'Och, Tommy, you can tell us,' Aunt Crissie persisted.

Tom lowered his head and shifted self-consciously in his chair.

'C'mon, Tom,' his mother encouraged him.

He looked up at them. Aunt Crissie was smiling at him.

'Is he going to say something?' she asked.

Tom looked towards her. He was frowning. Then slowly his face smiled as it was taken over by one of his huge grins. He looked at his father, as if for encouragement, before turning again to Aunt Crissie.

'I told him I would knock his balls in if he didn't stop messing about,' he said slowly and without a single stutter. 'Shughie'sss spoiled. All he needed was a gggood dig. That's all I sa sa said to hhhiim him.'

Martha, Joe and Aunt Crissie were speechless. Tom looked at each of them in turn, a little hesitantly at first. Then as his father winked slowly at him the bland, benign expression returned to his face. Joe started to laugh.

Tom's anxiety vanished and his face lit up at the sound. He looked again at his mother and Aunt Crissie and began to laugh also as he watched the looks on their faces. He turned again to his father and winked slowly in return.

The Curse of Emigration

Andrew McGovern

THE GIRL SAT on a chair in the middle of the kitchen floor. Neighbours joined hands and formed a circle around her. Everybody sang 'Now is the hour When we must say goodbye.'

Born in 1933 into a rural district of County Leitrim, I grew up in an environment where children were in abundance. We would all help at the various tasks on our parents' farms. One girl who shared work with our family was Helen O'Reilly. A few years older than me, she was like a big sister, only better. She never scolded me for any of my wrongdoings; rather, she would encourage me to be more of a brat than I was already.

In that era nobody told children anything about the facts of life. One got one's information from older children or from observing the animals on the farm. But we could not envisage our parents taking part in this flamboyant exercise. At eleven or twelve years of age I found myself relying on Helen for information about this taboo subject called *sex*. She would tell me about her boyfriends and the antics that they got up to. She would laugh her head off, saying, 'Andy, you will know it all soon enough. Just be patient.'

I really enjoyed working with Helen at the hay, turf or planting the potatoes. She was a good-looking girl, her auburn hair growing down her back in a mass of ringlets, and all her body shapes in the right places.

I would be sent along with her to 'gugger' (putting the seed into the holes made by the *stibhín*, a homemade tool with a long handle and pointed at one end). A peg was inserted nine inches from the pointed end and, with one's foot applied to this peg, a hole was made in the prepared ridge. Helen would stabilise each seed with the point of the *stibhín* and then we would move on to another row. It was a slow, tedious and time-consuming task, but the wit, humour and storytelling made it all bearable.

Now and then Helen would say: 'Sit there now until I get back.'

'Where are you going?' I would inquire.

'I'm going to make my water and you don't follow me now, yeh little monkey, yeh! Yeh know, Andy, nobody can ever stop wind or water!'

When I heard the rumour that Helen was to be off to America I had a cold feeling in my stomach, for I had depended so much on this girl for knowledge that she was my stepping-stone into the adult world. Already, by talking to her and working with her, I had developed confidence in myself and had no problems about talking to, or associating with, other girls. However, I knew that the preparations for going to America would take some time, so I would talk to Helen as much as I could before her emigration.

Finally, as I was approaching my fifteenth year, the day of Helen's departure arrived. My father told me, 'You'll have to go to that dance in O'Reilly's tonight and, anyway, it's time you started going to dances'. So I dressed for this great occasion, shaving off the few black hairs on my lip, hoping that it might encourage a few more to sprout. With a spring in my step, I set off for O'Reilly's. The house was full: all the neighbours, young and old, were there. It was a sad occasion, and Helen was the first of this family of ten children to go. A lone fiddler rasped away at his instrument, trying to get it in tune with the accordion.

Finally, they started to play 'The Moon Behind The Hill'. The tapping sound of their feet on the cement floor was much louder than the music. Nevertheless, the audience got into better humour and a few people started to dance. Later, blue-rimmed mugs of tea were passed around, followed by plates of loaf bread and raspberry jam and, finally, sweet cake.

I sat quietly in the corner, taking part in nothing except my duty to the sweet cake. This was my first night out among adults and I was prepared to take it all in. A beautiful girl from a nearby village, a relative of Helen, was present. She was in her early twenties, scantily dressed but full of confidence and, no doubt, attracting the attention of every young male there. She moved through the crowd, talking to every young man but not staying long with any of them, much to their great disappointment. Then she came across the floor in my direction. 'She must be going to talk to the man sitting beside me or the musician on my left.' I thought. But what a shock I got when she bent down beside me and said, 'Well, Andy?'

The next thing I knew, she had her arms around my neck and was kissing me. Yes, me. This was no peck on the cheek, as her moist lips pressed hard against mine. The crowd cheered and laughed. I was absolutely mortified but I did not resist. At least, while this kiss continued, I was sheltered from the peeping eyes. Nobody could see my face and it gave me time to regain my composure. At last, alas, she released me, stood upright, and enquired, 'How did you like that, Andy?'

'It was all right,' I stuttered.

She moved on, laughing. I felt like kicking her up the arse, to help her on her way, but I knew that this would only draw more attention to my already humiliated state, so I smiled at everyone, rubbing the lipstick from my mouth. Later, I discovered that Helen's father had prompted this girl saying,

'That's an old-fashioned buck over there. It's high time someone gave him a kiss.'

Dancing and singing continued and soon daylight
appeared through the window on this June morning. Much
later, the sun appeared from behind a drumlin hill, its rays
dancing on the kitchen window. A hand reached up to the
globe of the paraffin-oil lamp and its light soon became
redundant. Then there came a hush in the kitchen. Someone
brought a wicker chair to the centre of the floor. Helen
moved in the direction of the chair and sat on it, smiling at
everyone around her and looking unconcerned. All joined
hands and then formed a circle around her. The singing started, 'Now is the hour When we must say goodbye'.

The room door creaked and Helen's mother was seen making her way to the bedroom, face in hands. Nevertheless, the
singing continued: *Soon you'll be sailing Far across the sea.*
Again the room door creaked, Helen's father was next and
the door was closed tight. Then, *While you're away Oh, then,
remember me, When you return You'll find me waiting here.*

Helen's head dropped, her auburn ringlets now spread out
over her knees, the ends of her hair wet with tears and her
shoulders shaking uncontrollably. But nobody went to comfort her. This was in keeping with the tradition of the 'The
American Wake'. The person emigrating should suffer this
humiliation before leaving home.

An urge built up within me. I could not stand it any longer,
I felt like breaking through the circle and clinging to Helen in
the chair. This was the girl who had taught me everything
about growing up. This was the girl who had planted our
potatoes and now, here was I watching her suffer

However, I refrained from breaking the circle. Had I not
been made a fool of already tonight? And, anyway, I was only
a brat of a gossoon. Maybe I was feeling sorry for myself and,
indeed, my loss was greater than hers. Came the last bar of
the song, *Now is the hour When we must say goodbye.*

People crowded to Helen. There were hugs, kisses, hand-shakes and claps on the back. I could hear voices say, 'We'll see you soon again', or 'I might be over there myself some day. But you'll come back a millionaire. Good luck, Helen; it's well for you!'

So many remarks came from so many people. I kept on the outside of the crowd and, as people were moving towards the door, I was brought with the flow, intentionally. I could not bring myself to say goodbye to Helen and, anyway, she wouldn't miss me. After all, I was only a brat of a gossoon!

Slowly, I walked the quarter of a mile home. Corncrakes galore were singing in the river meadows. A cuckoo flew past, accompanied by a smaller bird. This was my first night out as an adult. I should feel elevated but never felt as low in all my life. I had got a kiss that I didn't want; my first kiss, an unpleasant experience, and now the person that I depended on for so much was about to depart. But I would recover. As Helen once told me, 'Andy, never count the times you fall but count the times you get up.'

I never saw Helen again, nor did her parents, for she never returned from America where she married and had a family of her own.

Recently, I met the person who gave me that first kiss fifty-five years earlier. Now a woman in her mid-70s, I enquired from her, 'Do you remember the night that you gave me a kiss in O'Reilly's?' She paused for a moment, and said, 'I remember being in O'Reilly's at the American Wake, but I don't remember giving you a kiss.'

'You wouldn't, would yeh?' said I. 'It's a lot easier to remember the 'whillot' gotten (severe blow) than the 'whillot' given!'

Now and then, I pass by the deserted house that once was a beautiful, three-room, neatly thatched cottage, where ten children and their parents lived in the forties. The children have scattered and the old folk are gone. Ghost voices from the past echo to me from its ruins, 'Oh, Andy, stop and have a chat. You're grown-up, now. You're not a brat. Your memory is so clear of happenings in the past. Pick up your pen, and record this fast. Life is just a passing period of time, from the movement of the body, to the drawing of breath. From the pleasures of life, to the darkness of death.'

Amen, a Thiarna! (So be it, my God)

Night Visitor

Sr Clare Julian

THE OLD COTTAGE that is my sanctuary lies snugly tucked high into the green-shawled breast of an Irish mountain. The wide view takes the breath away; the loving hands of the Creator God have moulded it softly, and He has spread a green, tree-stitched patchwork softly over it and scattered snowflake sheep there.

And always the wide heavens, blue, grey, white, an ever-changing splendour.

This peace-filled place, a mile from my nearest neighbour, is where I spend my days as a Franciscan hermit-sister, in 'silence and solitude and persevering prayer', threading beads for rosaries, knitting, and weaving St Bridget's crosses, with just my three cats, all of Siamese extraction, for company. I go out only rarely, for mass and shopping. And in the intervening days I see no one.

And I watch the passing seasons unfold – spring just now, my first here. The daffodils I planted before the winter are unfurling their golden skirts to dance in their bright joy, and I am starting a new orchard and vegetable patch.

In this tree-filled place, the birds delight and enchant. I set up a platform and hung feeders from a sycamore tree within good sight of the south-facing door, and whenever it is fine enough, I take my handwork and prayers out there and watch them. Tiny, rainbow-bright jewels of God. Some follow me now when I climb the drive to the very top of the mountain where my mailbox is.

This is a traditional old cottage, so my bedroom leads off the main room, and I leave the door open to see the comforting flickering of the Sacred Heart lamp I had put in above the high old mantel. Last autumn, I had a plague of mice, but Mowgli-Mouse-Slayer caught one a day, until the rest of them fled up the drive, waving a white flag. Then, a few weeks ago, in a freezing February spell, I heard scrabbling from the main room.

The cats sleep in the hot press in the bathroom, the warmest place in the house, of course. So I left my snug bed and padded through to fetch him. And saw a strange sight.

I had left a pear and a few dates on the big polished table, but all that was left of my one pear was the woody stalk – and the date stones were scattered round it . . .

And the table was covered in sooty paw prints. I was intrigued!

I duly fetched Mowgli – about fourteen pounds of ginger purr with a loud Siamese voice – and retreated to bed.

The scrabbling soon started again.

'GO!' I whispered. The cat moved not a whisker.

I tried to push him off the bed, but he was superglued to it.

So I crept out of bed, through the doorway – and snapped on the light! A large brown critter froze, its back to me, near the hearth. Long, wide tail. Then it shot off back up the chimney, dropping the tooth marked apple it was carrying off.

I have a large internet mail contact list, mostly American – I am a thoroughly up-to-date sister, using this technology to do God's work. Folk asked if I was not scared; one said she would have been off down the mountain with all her possessions. Another wanted to come and fetch me 'back to civilisation'. But it never occurred to me to be frightened.

It was, from the paw prints, obviously not a rat, which would have had me running for cover.

And I was curious and delighted.

As I suspected, and as the internet soon told me, my hungry night visitor was a pine marten, 'the rarest and shyest of Ireland's mammals and very hard to find'. Not when you are a Franciscan hermit-sister. All you do is creep out of bed and there he is, sitting on your table in the middle of the night, munching his way through as much fruit as he can hold.

And I was deeply thankful Mowgli had had the sense to cling to my blankets. Pine martens are not aggressive – but if threatened, have powerful jaws. Wise, wise feline. The nights that followed were fascinating, if sleepless! I so longed to see him again, especially his face. So I left food in the hearth – including the apple he had dropped. Once or twice I sat up, wrapped in a blanket. But these critters never come when you want them. Then a few nights later, I was roused by a loud scratching. I stumbled out of bed, half asleep, to find it was coming from outside the front door.

There is little I am afraid of – but opening a door on a frenzied pine marten who seems bent on tunnelling through it at 2 a.m. does not seem a wise thing to do. And it was a full moon that night. Shouting availed naught, so I switched the outside light on. Silence! And opened the door to shout, 'USE THE CHIMNEY!' At these times I am glad I have no neighbours. He had made sizeable inroads on the doorpost, which I dowsed with pungent white spirit to protect it, and had left a neat row of fresh droppings.

A couple of nights later, when I had put a board up at the fireplace, needing sleep, I had left the light on by accident after my normal 4 a.m. foray for coffee before my prayer day starts. And there he was well after five, almost the very end of the night. And we looked at each other, before he adroitly shifted the board and fled.

Large nocturnal eyes; wonderful sight.

But it was then that I reread all the information with the eyes of compassion, for he had braved the light he was afraid of, and near day, too. That was sheer desperation.

He is a predator; and at this time of year, there is no prey. I remembered how net bird feeders had been stolen so that I always bring then in at night, too. And the scraped diggings in the woods.

Pine martens mate in August, but like seals and badgers, implantation is delayed and the pregnancy does not start until March, and they store food for winter, which must have been all gone at this harsh season. This was a creature near starving.

Hunger is a hard bedfellow. My heart went out to him, and from a novelty and a curiosity he became one of God's waifs in need of help. I should tell you that soon after I first came to Ireland, I gave my chicken stew dinner to some starving abandoned cats . . . and fed them for the six months I was there in Mayo. I fear I am a hopeless case.

I also thought back to when I bought the cottage. There was a large, round hole at the bottom of the front door – pine marten shaped. And once or twice when I was very new here, and the cats were with me, I was sure I heard an animal running round in the main room.

The cottage was empty for several years, so this became part of his territory. I am the intruder, not him. This was his home before it was mine.

He eats mice and rats, so he will help keep the place vermin free. Because he, like all God's creatures, has a planned and vital place in the natural ecology.

And has been hunted almost to extinction. Man is his only enemy.

In this place, he is safe, protected. 'And they shall not hurt nor harm on all God's holy mountain.' Or they will have one irate sister to deal with!

And I certainly never need worry about getting the chimney

swept! So we now have a good arrangement, the pine marten and I.

I leave food in the hearth every night, an eclectic mix: cat food (I had some tins that mine just will not eat), as he is a carnivore, carrot, apple and chunks of home made bread. He comes when he needs to and takes all he wants. I never hear him or see him.

It is not every night. He never comes in strong winds; I think he climbs a tree and leaps across, which is a great feat indeed. Flying pine marten. And he comes if it is very wet.

Folk wanted me to tame him. They said, 'You will soon have him eating out of your hand.' But he is a wild creature with his own dignity and identity and integrity; I would not thus degrade him, or make him unnecessarily dependent. He is, as I have seen, very capable of fending for himself and his family!

I am simply helping him through a bad patch. And I feel deeply privileged to be doing so.

If he wants to bring his family to meet me when they arrive (wonderful image!), I will be honoured indeed; but if he stops coming when spring arrives, that is fine, too.

And when I wake, warm and snug in my bed in the small hours, by the flickering glow of the Sacred Heart lamp, I think of that beautiful animal, curled up among the trees with his pregnant mate, maybe with that glorious tail wrapped round his nose as the cats do, fast asleep with a full tummy, and with food stored for the night ahead.

And I smile.

God is in His heaven, who made 'All things bright and beautiful', and all is well when we help Him and these His creatures who brighten this fair and fertile world He gave us.

And I remind myself that I had planned to take a break from caring for animals. But God has other ideas – so here I am, a Franciscan hermit-sister in an isolated hermitage high on a remote Irish mountain, with three cats, a few dozen birds, and a pine marten who comes down the chimney for food.

And I have the strangest feeling that this is just the beginning. And I am smiling!

You can visit Sister Clare at <u>www.angelfire.com/ny5/srclarejulian/</u>

Christmas with the Enemy

Michael J. Cox

IT WAS CHRISTMAS Eve 1944; I was just six years old – well, six and a half to be exact – and the world was at war. We lived in a market town close to the border, and, like most of the North, we were fortunate enough to escape most of the horrors of the war. Just a few miles out of town, however, a large country house reminded us of those horrors. It had been converted into a recuperation and convalescent hospital, taking in allied soldiers who had been wounded or seriously injured in action.

I lived with my grandparents at this time, as my parents were kept busy with the ancillary duties of war. My father was a volunteer ambulance driver, and my mother, who was a nurse, had volunteered for service in the emergency ward at the local hospital. My grandfather, whom I loved dearly, was an architect. He was a quiet man, very charitable, deeply religious and highly respected in the community. My grandmother was more politically inclined and had strong republican ideals.

There were two traditions in their house on Christmas Eve. The first was that my grandfather would leave the house at 7 p.m. with a box of festively wrapped bottles and would walk through the town with gifts and greetings for clients and friends. He would normally return at nine o'clock, at which time my great uncle, his wife and my cousins would join us for the second tradition – a huge Christmas Eve supper.

It was always an exciting time for me as I was allowed to stay up late to join them for the meal. On this particular night my grandfather was late returning. My grandmother was a bit anxious, but at about 9.30 p.m. we heard his key in door, accompanied by the noise of strange feet. We could see nobody, but we heard him say, 'Now, you go in here and wash up and I'll collect you in a few minutes.'

He appeared in the dining room, apologised for his late-ness, and then turned to my grandmother. 'Mam, can you set three more places? We have some guests.' A minute or so later he left the room and then returned accompanied by three young soldiers in full uniform. We were all stunned. Except me. I could hardly contain myself; there were three real soldiers in my home, fighting men whom I had seen in all the papers. Brave men who went out to fight with real guns. I was ecstatic. My grandmother did not share my enthusiasm, in fact she went pale. She hissed at my grandfa-ther, 'They're *English* soldiers'.

He merely said, 'They're somebody's sons.' To a six-year-old they seemed to be big men, but I later discovered that they were only about nineteen or twenty.

Grandfather explained to us that he had met the three lads outside a local café, counting their coins to see if they could afford to buy some fish and chips. They had all been recovering at the army hospital and were returning to active service in two days time, on Boxing Day – it seems they had been recalled to train for a big event scheduled for the New Year. This was their last night of freedom and, being non-drinkers, they hadn't been asked to join their colleagues for a wild party that was now in progress else-where in the town.

Despite my grandmother's reservations, she joined in the general conversation. We learned that their names were

Cyril, Roger and Martin, that all three were from the English Midlands, that all three had already seen action, and that all three had been severely wounded.

We tucked into our meal of cold meats and potato salad, and finished with plates of Granny's famous trifle. The adults had a bottle of wine and I had a large bottle of lemonade. In those days of rationing, the wine, like the food, had come from a mystical and magical place, which, I learned, was called the Free State.

As the three lads were all non-drinkers, I was asked to share my lemonade with them. This was my great moment; the real soldiers were drinking from the same bottle as me! They even smiled at me and asked questions. I was too dumbstruck to answer but thrilled that they should acknowledge me. Then came the toasts. My grandfather wished everyone a Happy Christmas and wished the three lads good fortune, but when it came to toasting Absent Friends, I suddenly grew up. For the first time in my short life I saw grown men cry.

The soldiers had to leave to catch their bus to the hospital. We all shook hands with them, except my grandmother who couldn't quite bring herself to do so, but she still had a tear in her eye as they walked out the door. I had shaken hands with real soldiers!

Off to bed. Thinking about the amazing evening, shaking the hands of real soldiers who had shared my lemonade, wondering at the tears and wondering what it was like to spend Christmas away from home.

I've thought of them occasionally since then. Did they survive their big event? Did they survive at all? Did they ever think about a six-and-a-half-year-old whose little life they had transformed? Did they remember a Christmas Eve in a nationalist home?

As he passed my room, my grandfather came in, sat on my bed, wished me a Happy Christmas, warned me to be asleep before Santa came, and then said, 'I don't think you should ever talk about the soldiers to anyone, ever.'

And I never have – until now!

The Eviction Bowsies

Bill Cullen

"AVICSHUN! AVICSHUN! THE Corpo are here for Missus Walsh! It's an avicshun!'

Mary Darcy opened her eyes and sat up listening. 'Did I hear "avicshun"?' she asked slowly.

Rita nodded just as the roar went up again: 'Avicshun! Avicshun! It's the Corpo for Missus Walsh.' With that, there was a loud bang of a door hitting the wall and the tramp of hobnailed boots on the stone hall.

Mary's face flushed red and she stood up, with anger in her eyes. 'Give me that poker, Rita,' she said, 'and Liam, you get that sweeping brush and come with me. You girls mind the little ones.' There was a pause as she retied her white apron around her swollen tummy and then took the poker and waved for Liam to follow her.

'I don't believe this,' she said. 'It can't be an avicshun in this day and age, in this kip of a house.' She opened the door and then leaned back to dip her fingers in the holy water font and blessed herself and sprinkled some water on her son. There were roars and screams coming up the stairs from Missus Walsh's room at the back of the hall. 'Let's go,' she said and down the stairs she went, with Liam behind her.

The Corporation had taken over the tenements years before from the profiteering landlords, who had evicted tenants left, right and centre for not paying their rent. But the

Corpo had a more charitable outlook, and evictions were now seldom seen. Only one had happened in the last twelve months, that had been at the top end of Summerhill, and the ould fella was moving on anyway. It was still a fearful sight to see the Corpo men throw every piece of his belongings out on to the footpath and leave him sitting there in the rain while they boarded up the doors and windows of the room. His brother arrived later that night with a horse and cart. They loaded up his bits and bobs and off they went, never to be heard of again.

When Mary turned the corner of the stairs, she saw three Corpo lads in the hall, with Missus Walsh's table and chairs already being handed out from man to man. Some children were standing barefoot in the hall crying, and she could hear Missus Walsh's voice from the room pleading tearfully, 'No, no, don't throw us out.'

Mary let out a roar – 'What's going on here, ya bowsies!' – and she smashed the poker on the banisters with a loud crash that brought the men to a halt. 'Who's in charge here?' she shouted, and out from the room came a big, red-faced man, followed by Mr Sutton, the rent collector.

'I'm in charge here, missus,' said the big man, in a country accent. 'Now you just buzz off and mind your business. This is an official Corporation eviction, and you'll be in the clink if you're not careful.'

Mary gave the banister another bang with the poker. 'Well, aren't you the big brave culchie now, threatening women and children, sneaking in here when our men are out working to pay your rent? If it's trouble you want, you've come to the right place, and I'm telling ya to leave Missus Walsh's things alone or you'll have me to deal with,' she shouted without taking a breath.

'And as for you, Mr Sutton, come out from hiding behind that culchie and speak up for yourself. Don't you know Mr Walsh was in hospital for a few months with the kidney stones. And he's back working now and they'll clear off the arrears. Don't ya know all that, and why are ya here with these latchicos doing your dirty work?'

Mr Sutton just blinked behind his glasses as the big man did the answering. 'Listen, woman, it's none of your business. He's had plenty of warnings. When any tenant falls behind by more than six months' rent, it's out. That's the policy and there's no discussion.' Turning to his men, he said, 'Right, me lads, let's get on with the job,' but before they could move Mary smashed the banister again with the poker.

'So that's the policy, is it now? Let's throw the sick man and his family out on the street is the policy, because they owe the Corpo a few lousy pounds. Let's get a big brave culchie up from Cork with his pals to dump them on the road. Sure they're well used to this job. Didn't some of ya help the English landlords during the famine days. Turncoats and informers ya are, who take on only the women and children. We'll leave the room there empty and put Missus Walsh out in the rain. Well, that's the policy we had when the Brits were here, and many's the brave Irishman's blood was spilt to get them out and change that policy. Is this what Michael Collins fought for? Of course, he was a great man from Cork, and he was shot in the back by one of his own. The like of you. Let me tell you this, me boyo – the first man that moves a stick of furniture out of this hall will get my poker over his head.'

What a tirade. The big Corkman was kicking the wall, saying, 'Feck ya! Feck ya! Feck ya!' Mary Darcy stood halfway up the stairs in her white apron, heavily pregnant, waving the poker, her face flushed with anger. Her young son stood beside her, with a sweeping brush held across his chest.

Mary came down the stairs into the hall and took a chair from one of the men, without resistance. 'Now, Mr Sutton,' she said, 'why don't you get these men out of here and let's see how we can clear off Missus Walsh's arrears. Sure, I've two pounds here in me pocket. Wouldn't that be a better thing to do than have some of these culchies in hospital. '

The big man was livid with temper at the insults that had been heaped on him. He would have killed any man who used those words to him, but he was helpless and frustrated when faced with a pregnant woman.

The rent collector broke the tension. 'Well, are you saying, Missus Cullen, that we can have the arrears paid?' he asked.

'Of course, I'm saying the arrears will be paid, Mr Sutton,' she replied. 'Get rid of these boyos and we'll sit down on these chairs and work everything out.'

'Right then,' said Mr Sutton, turning to the big man. 'You go on back to the office, Shamus, and I'll sort this out.'

The big man kicked the wall in frustration. 'Bejaysus, I'll go back to no feckin' office,' he said. 'I'll go down to Conway's pub, and you'll meet us there to pay us for our day's work, so you will.' And down the hall he went, with the sparks flying from his hobnailed boots. The other men put down the furniture and trailed out after him.

'Bring that stuff in now, Liam,' said the Ma, 'and why don't you put the teapot on, Missus Walsh. I'm sure Mr Sutton could do with a cuppa tea while we talk business.' Twenty minutes later, Mr Sutton left, with the promise of six shillings a week payment off the arrears as well as the rent from next week on. Missus Walsh didn't know where she'd get the extra money from.

'Don't worry about that, Missus Walsh. We've won the haggle today, and we can win it again if need be,' said Mary, she left to go back upstairs.

Vera and Rita had been watching the commotion from the landing. When Mary arrived back, it was to a steaming mug of tea and a slice of toast ready for her on the table. She smiled at them all and sat down. 'Isn't it a great bunch I have here now. The girls looking after the house and this young fella standing in for his da,' she said, ruffling Liam's curly black hair. 'You can put this poker and that brush of yours away now, son,' she said.

But as she sipped her tea, she grimaced and said, 'Liam, run down and tell Mother Darcy to come up here quick, and Vera, will you put that big pot of water on the stove.'

That evening, Carmel was born in the tenement room. The children had all been hooshed down to stay in Molly's. When they trooped back for bed, Mary was sitting up with the new baby and Billy was there beside her. Mother Darcy was having a mug of shell cocoa; she had a proud look on her face and her sleeves were still rolled up. 'Mother Darcy brought the new baby up from the chapel in her shopping bag,' was the story Rita gave.

The Da was back in Brooks Thomas, but only part-time. He got the odd few days' work with his brother Jack in Granby Pork Products. Granby's were up in Granby Lane at the back of Dominick Street Church, beside the rear of Walden Ford Dealers. At other times, he worked as an usher in the picture houses: the Plaza in Granby Row and the Rotunda Cinema at the Parnell Monument. His military training was great for keeping the queues of children under control, and he was meticulous in his cleanliness for the butcher's. But he'd no work coming up to the Christmas, and the markets had a lean spell for Mary, who was still nursing her new baby, Carmel. The rain was seeping in around the tenement windows, and Billy had used up bundles of *Heralds* plugging the cracks to keep the draughts out.

One day his old army pal Johnny Coleman had dropped in with six army greatcoats. 'You have to keep these children of yours warm in bed, Mary,' he said, 'and these are just the job.' The coats went over the thin blankets and were a god-send for the kids.

'Snug as a bug in a rug you are now,' said Mary.

'Don't mention bugs, Mary,' Billy said. 'I've spent the last week fighting the clocks and spiders coming in these damp walls. The powder I got down in Con Foley's Medical Hall seems to be working. It's certainly done the job on the oul' mattresses, because I haven't seen a hopper since I doused them.'

Mary was quiet as she rocked the baby's cot. 'We'll have to get out of here, Billy, before this bloody place takes another of our babies. Have you heard anything from the Corpo? Mick Mullen put in a word for us, and he told me that with seven kids now, we should be getting an offer of a place soon.'

Billy looked at her and said, 'No, I haven't seen Mick, but I'll go and find him in Liberty Hall tomorrow. And I've to see Alfie Byrne next Tuesday.' Mary didn't respond. She just kept rocking the baby's cot.

'Jack has promised me some corned beef and pigs' feet for Christmas,' Billy continued. 'It'll make a fine dinner for the kids. They love the trotters.' It was no use. She was away somewhere else. So he just undressed and went to bed. Hours later, he woke. Mary was at the table darning some of the children's ganseys, singing her song in a low voice as she rocked the cot with her foot:

Somewhere over the rainbow,
Skies are blue,
And the dreams
That you dare to dream, really do come true.

The Beardy Man

Michael Carragher

On my mother's Dead List, Michael O'Brien comes right after Pope John and President Kennedy, so he must have died in the winter of 1963–64. But he was around for a while after his memorable first arrival.

'Mammy, Mammy! There's a beardy man coming up the loanen!' My mother dusted flour off her hands and hurried to the door. We clung to her as she faced him in the laneway: a stoutish man of middle height, with a fresh complexion and a ginger beard. 'Hello, ma'am. Could I trouble you for a bite to eat, please?' A seesaw accent. No local man. My mother was wary on that first meeting. Tramps and gypsies, as you could call them then, were more commonplace in country districts in the 1960s. Distrusted by many. And this was a *beardy man,* his barbaric appearance a cause for alarm in itself. Yet he hadn't begged for money, and there was no whining self-pity in his voice, no shifty glances round the yard or through the door. He might be ragged but he was clean. A good-looking man in middle age. And he was hungry. There but for the grace of God go any of the children clinging to a mother's skirts.

He ate the bread and drank the tea that Mammy brought him on the doorstep, muttering earnestly to the food as he devoured it. We children gawked from the kitchen, fascinated by that beard more than by the strange one-sided conversation. It was the first real beard we'd ever seen.

After that we were to see it almost every week. Michael's visits were part of an ancient pattern, then giving way to the expectations vested in a welfare state, and social and technological changes. Once such a man of the road would have been welcomed for the news he brought from far-flung places. But we had a wireless, and more recently a van. Daddy worked in Dundalk. We weren't starved for news. Still, we welcomed Michael. Once he brought a fiddle and played us jigs and reels. What increasingly impressed my mother, with her post-Victorian values, was his 'respectability'. He kept himself clean, stripping to the waist and washing vigorously at the pump; he was polite; and, in a time when people were more concerned with their responsibilities than mindful of their rights, he 'knew his place': he held to the doorstep even when he would have been made welcome in the kitchen, moving to the narrow porch in the rain.

He accepted with easy gratitude my father's cast-off shirts then ripped the collars off immediately. Perhaps he was simply uncomfortable in the newfangled sewn-in collars; or perhaps he had too much respect for the collar and tie to wear a collar himself now. Michael had known better times. He had trained as a solicitor in Cork but had lost his position through drink. Whether he still drank I don't know, but we never saw the sign of it on him, and he never asked for money. He may have exorcised that demon.

For a couple of years he was part of our lives. Every Saturday he would call. So when two, then three, then four weeks passed without him, our curiosity turned to dark presentiment. Eventually came news of decomposed remains found near Ballymascanlon. 'It must be poor Michael,' Mammy said sadly. And so it proved. All she could do for him now was add his name to the list that began 'For Granny and Granda', and ended 'and all the Souls in Purgatory', a list that grew inexorably as relatives and loved ones died. On that long list our old tramp's place is next to a president and a pope.

The Wheelchair

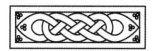

Leslie Dawes

THE YOUNG MAN wearing a navy blue tracksuit leant over the wall of the Reaghlough stone bridge. He scanned the empty railway line, which stretched out from underneath him. Then he took a mobile phone out of his pocket, carefully picked at the numbers, put it to his ear. There was a slight pause . . .

'Boss, Barry Morgan here. Sorry, there's no story – no bloody sign of this woman, supposed to be stuck in a wheelchair on the railway line. You sure your contact wasn't having you on?' There was a short pause. 'Yeah . . . Okay! Christine Keenan is her name. I'll ask if anybody has seen her. Don't forget I still have a stack of papers to deliver around Drogheda.' He switched off the phone and shoved it back into his hip pocket.

As he took a final look at the line, a sheet of newspaper suddenly fluttered out from underneath the bridge. He quickly slid down the embankment and landed feet first on the line. He spotted Christine in the wheelchair. She was in her early twenties, a small, intense woman, with a coat draped over her shoulders. She was parked right in the path of the noon express, bound for Belfast. Sheets of a newspaper were strewn at her feet.

Barry, anxiously: 'Miss, unless you get your arse off this line you're going to be mown down by the Southern Express, due through here at any minute.'

Christine, calmly: 'Why don't you pick up those pages and put them together . . . So I can continue to catch up with the headlines?'

Barry: 'That's what you'll be bloody well making it if you don't shift yourself . . . You wouldn't happen to be Christine Keenan, would you?'

Christine nodded her head: 'How do you know my name?'

Barry: 'I'll fill you in later. By the way, my name's Barry Morgan. Now why don't we shift you out of here?'

She glared at him, then settled back with a determined look on her face. 'Why?' she asked.

Barry, sharply: 'Why what – because you're soon going to close your account with fucking living if you don't.'

Christine: 'I don't. I've already told you, I'm not moving. I've a date . . .'

Barry, interrupting: 'You've got a bloody date with death.'

Christine: 'And I intend to keep it.'

Barry looked alarmed: 'Whoa, whoa, easy, miss. What are you saying? You've parked yourself deliberately on this fucking line to write yourself off?'

Christine: 'Got it at last! Now, be a good little Boy Scout, go and find somebody else to save.'

Barry: 'I've got one, right?'

Christine, glaring at him: 'Wrong! . . . Just leave me alone.'

Barry: 'Seems like I've got a fucking a nut case on my hands.'

Christine: 'Not a nut case – a protester. I want people to see me – ask why I'm parked under this bloody bridge.'

Barry looked puzzled: 'You've got up your hump . . . you're going to wrap yourself around the front of a train because people can't see you?'

Christine nodded her head: 'You don't see me. Do you know what happens when I roll down the street in Drogheda? I almost have to ask people to get out of my way.

Sometimes they open doors for me, but they're always looking three feet over my head. That's where my face would be
if I were a normal person. When they bother to notice me at
all, they talk to me like I was an idiot. I'm not a handicapped
person. I'm Christine Keenan, and I want to be recognised as
an individual. I want to make the public aware that people
like me do exist – even if it means having to spread myself
all over the front of a train!'

Barry: 'Jeez, that's no way to talk . . . You honestly think
that killing yourself will make a fart of difference? Most of
them are too busy, leading their own lives.'

Barry moved towards her and put his hands on the wheelchair and tried to push it. She turned quickly. 'You try that
and you'll be in serious trouble. Get away from me!'

He tried it again, and she suddenly produced a small can
of gas out of her pocket and pointed it at his eyes. 'Don't be
a fool!' she said.

Barry: 'Sure, Okay! Okay,'

Christine: 'This stuff is deadly . . . it'll blind you.'

Barry: 'Okay . . . I said I heard you, didn't I?'

Christine: 'Stand over there!'

Barry, edged nervously to the side of the tunnel: ' Okay,
just cool down. Let's jaw – not war. I'm not going to be any
good if I'm blind, am I?'

Christine: 'You won't be as long as you don't try that
again.'

Barry was now near the end of his patience. There was a
pause. Then he slowly put his hands behind his back and
tried to slip the mobile phone out of his pocket, but she was
too quick for him. 'It's rude to make a phone call when
you're talking to a lady,' she said. 'Just give me the phone,
and no more playing games with me.'

He handed over the phone. 'Look, miss,' he said, 'you're
not the only one who has the weight of the fucking world
leaning on you. It was on mine a few months ago. It was the

same old story – boy falls in with bad company. Boy becomes a piss artist. Boy becomes a lazy, good-for-nothing bastard, and headed for an early grave. Boy now in real bad trouble – until his lucky piece turned up.'

Christine is puzzled: 'Lucky piece?'

Barry: 'Dear old Bill Osborne – he was my lucky piece! He owns and edits *The Recorder*. He saved me from falling into hell. He kicked my arse out if it . . . made me see sense. "Don't run away from it, Barry," he said. "Don't be a coward. Fight it! Come and work for me. I need somebody to drive the delivery van. Let's see if we can straighten you out." Thinks a lot of me, he does!'

Christine: 'Did he straighten you out?'

Barry: 'He did up to a week ago! Then, I fell in with some of my old mates and been juiced up ever since – at least, until today.'

Christine: 'I bet Old Bill was angry?'

'His words hit me like a body blow,' said Barry. 'Told me straight that I'd no future with his paper. I stood stunned. I felt like telling him to stick the fucking paper up his arse – would have done in the old days. But I pleaded with him to give me one more chance, and he said he'd think about it.'

Christine: 'Well, I can't believe that you'd blow another opportunity because you can't keep your mouth away from demon drink?'

'Yeah, well that's every alco's problem. We've good days and bad days – just one mouthful on a bad day and we're back in hell.' Then he suddenly goes quiet and thinks to himself. 'Perhaps I should be helping her to die? Hell, what a great story, what a scoop? – An interview with a young crippled woman, just seconds before she throws herself in front of the express? A real shocker! Old Bill will love it. There'd be no more talk about giving me the sack.'

Christine looked at him, wondering why he was so quiet. He panicked a bit, and asked himself, 'What if the police accuse me of not trying to save her? But that'll be no problem. I'll just tell them she kept this canister of gas pointed at my eyes and threatened to use it if I tried to push her off the line. Yeah, she was determined to die, and there was nothing I could have done to stop her.'

Christine bit her lip and stiffened. She cried a little in spite of herself and tried to keep Barry from seeing it. 'Sorry to go soft on you,' she said. 'Looks as if we could both do with some spiritual guidance. Doesn't matter now. It's too late. I'm sorry we didn't meet yesterday. Then things might have been different. Anyway, you'll have a good story to tell – I hope you'll write it from my point of view?'

Barry glanced at his wristwatch, considered, then reached a decision. He was now confused, clearly moved by her tears, her plight and her beauty, which he was seeing for the first time. He moved on to the line and attempted to sit down beside her. 'There's not even a minute to go,' he said calmly. 'Give me a little space?' He sat down.

Christine: 'For God's sake, Barry, please, go away. Old Bill won't give you the sack – not after you bring back my story . . . Now you've a nice life, providing you stick to the alcoholics' bible, and have every right to live it. I'm dead from the neck down, a useless misfit, and have every right to die.'

Barry: 'Crap! If you're going to stay here, I want to stay with you,'

Christine: 'Why?'

Barry suddenly bent down, pulled her to him and kissed her gently. As he released her, she looked at him, with a love now clearly in her eyes.

Barry: 'That's why . . . If the train's going to trash you, I want it to trash me, too.'

She was now almost in tears. 'You know you're screwing up everything, don't you? You know bloody well you and me would never work out. You couldn't handle me. I'd be like a millstone around your neck!'

Barry, smiling: 'Life's full of screw-ups! You get a nice little number going, and somebody comes along and fucks it up. You meet someone special, and your whole world is turned upside down. It's happened to me – I was going to let you die so I could write a big story about you. It's a bastard, but it happens!'

Christine: 'Do you know how dumb, stupid but lethally true you sound?'

Barry: 'Sorry – but at least I've proved that I see you . . . Anyway, what kind of fucking rat would let a pretty young girl like you die, just to save his fucking job?'

There's a pause. 'How long?' she asked.

'Any second,' he replied

Barry turned to Christine and looked her directly in the eyes as he extended his hand . . . 'Hi,' he whispered.

She took his hand and gripped it tightly . . . 'Hi,' she whispered. She desperately now wanted him to want to be with her.

As they waited, they heard the sound of the approaching train. He desperately threw his arms around her. There was a deafening roar as it rushed through, leaving bits of the wheelchair scattered to either side of the line.

A short time later, as old Bill Osborne sat at his desk in *The Recorder* newsroom, the phone disturbed him. He grabbed it, put it to his ear. As he listened, he felt a chill at his heart. 'Jeez. I don't believe it!' he said. 'Young Barry's been killed – by an express train? What happened?' There was a pause as he listened. His expression then changed to shock. 'He's a fucking hero?' he asked. He searched for further suitable words but couldn't find any . . .

'Yes, he died, saving my life,' replied the voice at the other end. 'I'm Christine Keenan. I'm the crippled girl in the wheelchair!'

Having a Ball

Carmel Wynne

It's very hard to get a ticket for the All-Ireland Hurling finals in Croke Park from the Gaelic Athletic Association. The demand always far outstrips the supply, so you can understand what wonderful expectations were raised in the Murphy family when their twelve-year-old daughter Máire won two stand tickets. Everyone in the family knew that Máire had no interest in hurling or camogie. She was a kind-hearted girl who loved people and those who were close to her knew that she wouldn't keep the tickets. Some expected that she would give the tickets away, others believed that she would sell them and give the money to charity and others still said she might raffle them; that way she would make even more money for charity.

The question of what was going to happen to young Máire's tickets was a major topic of conversation throughout the village. Her parents made no effort to influence her decision. Her two brothers, neighbours and fellow pupils pondered and speculated. Her classmates told Ms Byrne, their teacher, that her father was certain to get one. Her mother, like Máire, had no interest in sport although both of her brothers played hurling.

Neighbours enjoyed speculating. Would one of her two brothers be picked or would she give the ticket to someone else? How would she choose? A trip to Dublin for the

All-Ireland finals would be a dream come true for many young teenagers. When Máire finally announced that she wanted to give one ticket to her father and the other to 'Oul Johnny', a returned emigrant, her brothers were naturally disappointed. Her teenage brother Sean was most upset. 'That's not fair. He knows nothing about the game,' Sean complained. 'He doesn't even follow a team and I doubt if he could tell a goal from a point.' Her older brother Matt was more accepting of her decision. 'Look,' he said to Sean, 'you and I will have lots of opportunities to go to other hurling matches. We have our lives before us; Johnny is 70 years young. He doesn't need to know anything about hurling to enjoy the match – he'll have a ball.'

Johnny was thrilled when Máire surprised him with the invitation to go to the final with her father. He had never been to Croke Park before. It was a highly competitive game between Clare and Tipperary. Tipperary scored first and Johnny cheered madly, throwing his hat in the air. A few minutes later Clare scored. Johnny again cheered and threw his hat in the air. Máire's father smiled as a man behind them tapped Johnny on the shoulder. 'Don't you know what team you are supporting?' he asked. 'Me?' replied Johnny, visibly excited. 'Why, I'm not here to support any team. My young friend Máire gave me the ticket because she wanted me to have a good time. I'm just here to enjoy the game.'

The Challenge

Russ McDevitt

I HAD RUN out of money the morning I hitch-hiked into Townsville in Queensland. The town appeared deserted. Dogs lay in the shade panting with the heat. The only place open was an empty bar with the owner stacking empty beer barrels out back. He seemed taken aback on spotting me.

'We're not open for business yet, mate,' he said.

'It's okay, I'm not looking for a drink right now.'

I looked around me. 'Where is everybody? I haven't seen a single soul in town so far but yourself.'

He laughed. 'That's 'cause today is the Royal Show out at the show grounds. The whole town closes down for it.'

My face must have reflected my puzzlement. He stopped working and looked closer at me. 'You're not from Aussie, are you? What were you looking for in Townsville anyway?'

'Well, I'm from Ireland and I been hitch-hiking up through Queensland. I could use some work. Anything going right now?'

He made a face. 'The only work around here is cane cutting, and that's done by the Italians. Believe me, working in the heat and dirt would kill you or me in half a day.'

He paused rubbing his chin. 'You know, probably the best thing you could do is go out to the Royal Show and try to get some work on some of the sideshows. They travel all over Queensland and are always looking for people.' He squinted at me. 'They're a rum lot, though; you need to be able to look after yourself.'

With this warning ringing in my ears, I walked a mile to the showgrounds.

What a change from the silent deserted town! Hundreds of people milling around, young and old, engaged in having fun as only Australians can. It featured some rides I'd never encountered before, including a rodeo with bucking broncos and bulls, and the dance of the seven veils with some intriguing banners outside. A warning from Father O'Malley echoed in my head about 'the sins of the flesh' and I quickly moved on.

A large crowd was milling round a massive marquee that featured a platform in front with what appeared to be boxers standing on it. One of these was hammering on a drum while two others were energetically ringing large bells. Behind them hung pictures of famous boxers, flapping in the breeze. The heading on the banners stated boldly: 'JIMMY SHARMEN'S BOXING STADIUM'.

A tough-looking young man wearing a bush hat emerged from the marquee and climbed up a ladder to where the boxers stood. The crowd fell silent as he reached the centre of the platform and picked up a microphone. 'Folks, I'm Jimmy Sharmen. On behalf of the fighters on the board, I am throwing out challenges to anyone on your showground today with the heart, pluck, courage and ability to stand up to a stipulated number of rounds with any athlete on the board. We will undertake to stop, knock down, make squib or give up anything from eight stone to one ton! Come on, where's your local and district champions?'

With that he shut up and the drum and bells picked up their crescendo again. The crowd grew even larger, and I was squeezed in even closer to the platform. Sharmen raised his microphone again.

'Let me introduce you to some of our fighters, folks.' Here

he started calling the boxers individually up to the centre of the line-up board. His introductions had his own special brand of Australian humour, which the crowd loved.

'Here's a kid who came into our campfire one night starving. We gave him a book on boxing to read which he promptly ate, and he's never looked back since. We call him the Rum Jungle Kid, and he'll beat anything on two or four legs out there under eight stone. Now, let's see some hands from you young bucks out there. Who wants to try to go three rounds with the kid? If you do, we'll give you a fiver.'

In this fashion Sharmen quickly matched up two fighters and the challengers climbed up the ladder, were quickly interviewed by him and stood alongside the person they had agreed to fight. At this point Sharmen raised his hand again and the crowd fell silent.

'Look, sports, as I mentioned already we put on three exciting bouts with every house. Now we've got fighters I want to introduce our wrestler Paul Marino, the Maori from New Zealand, over here to warm-up for the season.' A solid looking, copper-coloured man eased his way past the boxers to the centre while the drum and bells rang out again.

The Maori took off a light colourful jacket he was wearing and posed for the crowd. The crowd murmured appreciatively, and a few catcalls came flying up, mainly from women. He looked pretty formidable and wore a somewhat disdainful expression as he looked out at the crowd.

Sharmen cut in again. 'Now look, sports, I'm paying Paul Marino big money just to have him with us, so I want him to do some work for his money – and he's getting soft, too! Today I'm offering a tenner to anyone who can last three rounds with him. Come on, I know Townsville is a place that breeds 'em tough. Let's see some hands up here.'

The drum and bells rang out again.

I was chatting to two men alongside me and leaned forward to shout over the noise. 'You know, I used to do some wrestling.' The drum and bells had just fallen silent at that moment and my voice seemed to echo loudly. Next minute I was grabbed by the two men, who pushed me over to the ladder. One shouted, 'We got a guy here who'll kill the Maori!' And they pushed me half up the ladder.

Sharmen leaned forward, his face close to mine. 'Where are you from, son?'

'Ireland,' I stammered.

'Look, son,' he roared into the mike, 'if the Maori gets you in his flying mare, he'll fire you all the way back to Ireland. If he tears your back leg off and hits you across the skull with it, don't come screaming to me for compensation!'

With that I attempted to climb down the ladder, but the crowd pushed me back up, and the next moment I ended up on the line-up board standing next to the Maori champion. He seemed bigger close up and looked suitably unimpressed with my appearance. The brief interview by Sharmen was a blur, and I found myself down in a changing room wearing a borrowed pair of shorts and runners. Dimly I listened to the crowd roaring for blood inside where the two boxing bouts were taking place. I couldn't help thinking, 'McDevitt, this is another nice mess you've got yourself into.'

The last boxing match seemed to finish very quickly and they came to get me. Inside I was surprised to discover that there was no ring at all, just two massive tent poles and a square of light canvas on the ground with no padding. You could see the outline of stones sticking up from the hard-baked Australian soil. The crowd stood around the square of canvas, hemming in tightly. Sharmen introduced us both briefly and the bell went.

I'd love to be able to relate a story of courage and over-coming adversity, but the truth is that the Maori nearly killed me!

I'd learned some wrestling moves in Canada where, in the gym, your partner worked along unagressively with you and in effect jumped over as you attempted to throw him. Unfortunately the Maori had never done this course. He initially looked puzzled at my puny efforts but then started picking me up and hurling me into the crowd. Then he'd stroll into the crowd, pick me up and hurl me back into the centre of the ring, where I became acquainted with, it seemed, every rock outlined through the canvas. Later I was told that my best technique was trying to climb the tent poles in an attempt to avoid the Maori's clutch!

After two rounds I gasped to Sharmen, who came over to my corner to check on me, 'I can't go on, I've had it. I'm absolutely knackered!'

His head snapped back. 'We can't stop it now, the crowd love you. They'll tear this place apart!' He patted me on my shoulder. 'Let me have a chat with the Maori, maybe he'll work along with you for the last round.'

With that he darted across to the opposite corner where he was engaged in what seemed to be heated argument with the Maori. In a moment he was back. 'Paul's going to ease up and work along with you. Just go out there and have a real go at him. This has got to go the distance.'

I suddenly got new heart and found that some of my throws were actually working. I was throwing the Maori all over the place. The crowd went wild! I got a bit carried away and ran the Maori's head into the tent pole. Fortunately the bell rang just then as he got up with murder in his eyes.

The crowd gathered into the centre of the ring. 'Pay him his tenner,' they screamed. I found out later that some of the boxing troupes had a reputation for not paying up when one of their fighters got beaten. Sharmen peeled some bills off a large roll and handed them to me.

The crowd lifted me onto their shoulders and took me off to the nearest beer tent where I spent the only money I had left in the world.

Hours later, I came back to the boxing tent where I had left my rucksack. They had had two more shows since the one I was involved in, and the fighters and hands were busy folding up sidewalls and throwing tent poles into trucks. I found Jimmy Sharmen sitting in his caravan.

He grinned at me. 'You did pretty good today, cobber. How would you like to do that every day?'

'Every day! Sorry, I don't follow you.'

'Well, hey look, you're knocking round Australia, we're on the road for part of the year. Why don't you join us?'

'Join you, doing what?'

'Just doing what you did today. Come in carrying your rucksack and challenge the Maori.'

'Are you kidding? It feels like every bone in my body is bruised and battered, and that's just after one fight. You might as well feed me to the sharks right now.'

Sharmen laughed uproariously. 'I'm not suggesting that you duplicate today's effort again. You and the Paul can work out a routine just like the third round today. No one needs to get hurt. My problem is that no one wants to come in and wrestle him.'

'Well, I can tell you why if you're interested,' I said bitterly.

Sharmen looked speculatively at me. 'Here, I'll tell you what. We're working our way up the coast to Cairns and then coming back down to the Brisbane Royal Show where we're going for seven straight days. We need an extra wrestler for this. You could learn the routine by then and probably quite a lot about wrestling. At Brisbane you could make some good money to help with your trip, and in the meantime we'll feed you. How about it?'

And that's what we did. Most of it worked out as Sharmen had predicted. A hitch occurred when I was standing in the crowd in Cairns confidently challenging the Maori when I became aware of another wrestler in the crowd. A real challenger! A docker who actually carried a docker's hook in his belt.

Sharmen's solution was a surprise – to me! He matched me and the docker, with the winner to meet the Maori.

While a bit more streetwise by then, I still became reacquainted with all the hard rocks under the canvas and barely survived getting hurt, but it served a purpose; the Maori had a chance to study his style and beat him in the next house. I was now acting as a buffer for Paul Marino!

And so it was for a while, moving around the country from one show to another and learning another valuable lesson of life – never take things at face value. They are not always as they appear.

The Flyer

Michael Fox

'FOR THE PEOPLE *that went, for the people that came back, for the people that stayed.*' Those words are from a plaque in Bohola, County Mayo.

Bohola is a very pretty and neat village, partially bypassed by the N5 trunk road and the turn-off for one of the 'winding roads to Kiltimagh'. One of Bohola's claims to fame is, of course, that it is home to the 'three pubs', originally known as McDonagh's, Clarke's and Roche's, the inspiration for Mayoman Michael Commins' song 'Three Pubs in Bohola'. In fact, the casual visitor or passer-by might be forgiven for concluding that, at first glance, the village consists only of three pubs. On previous occasions I have visited all three of them, a particularly memorable visit being when, inadvertently, I gatecrashed a funeral gathering at Clarke's, but was made most welcome!

More recently I made a detour to inspect Bohola's latest claim to fame – *The Flyer,* a sculpture representing a reflection on, not only the mass emigration from Bohola and surrounding districts in poorer times, but also on those that remained behind, and those that were able to come back; all *fliers* in their own way.

I found *The Flyer* – resembling to me, variously, a 'T', a figure with arms outstretched as if flying, a figure offering a welcoming embrace and a cross – perched on a grassy mound in a newly landscaped area in the centre of the village. Perhaps it is significant that the figure faces the main road out of the village for (and back from) Knock Airport, Dublin and beyond, with the local church and the infamous three pubs forming a backdrop.

An adjacent granite rock bears two metal plaques. The first reveals that the sculptor of *The Flyer* is Tim Morris, with sponsorship from local Bohola man William Durkin, and that the Mayo County Council Millennium Sculpture Initiative has managed the whole project. It was the second plaque that got my attention though. The words on the inscription evoke a keen sense of sadness, while describing strength of spirit and a 'bond' with the homeland:

THE FLYER: A SYMBOL FOR BOHOLA

One of the central conditions of life for Irish people, especially in the west, has been the necessity of flight for sons and daughters, and less often in the past, more often thankfully in the present, their return. As if a kind of forced aviation both deprived a district of their progeny, and yet called them back with all the power and poetry of place. The sons and daughters of the west, of Mayo itself, of Bohola, may have travelled far, but the secret music of their hearts hears always the magical notations of their home district. And the poignancy of the true work, the faithfulness, of those that remain also contains a kind of flight, the soaring of the soul when after great toil some vision of the western heavens opens, and the home place is revealed in all its mystery and majesty. Even those long living in the cities of Ireland, Europe and America, even after generations have passed, still carry this central essence of the home place, the extraordinary statement in the inner self of both staying and leaving, stillness and flight. It is the sum of these human experiences that constitutes a place like Bohola, in the setting of its beauty and its challenge, its reality and its dream. This sculpture wants to honour, mirror, and express that essence, to say the sentence of a place, to sing the hidden song of this enduring locale.

For the people that went, for the people that came back, for the people that stayed.

– Sebastian Barry

Unlike so many sculptures, *The Flyer* was not imposed on Bohola. The local community were very much involved with the project, with the local school having a particular interest to the extent that older pupils were invited to compose poetic pieces about it and what it represents. The three best have been inscribed upon metal plaques, along with the names of the pupils concerned, and these have been imbedded in the ground adjacent to the rock with the plaque bearing the above inscription, for posterity, along with *The Flyer.*

Moved by what I had seen, in the knowledge of the enforced emigration of many of my own family and ancestors, it occurred to me that, perhaps, *The Flyer* also has a message for me, and others like me of Irish descent, returning to the land of our fathers.

The next time you are in the vicinity, call into Bohola and take the opportunity of paying a visit to *The Flyer;* hopefully you, too, will gain some inspiration from what it represents. A visit to the three pubs might also assist in this regard!

The Emigrant

Tom Higgins

I'm over here in London
I'm here these forty years
I can't shut out fond memories
I can't keep back the tears

I miss my wife and family
I miss my friends at home
I am so lonely over here
No matter where I roam

I haven't got a shilling now
I'm always on the brink
For I got fond of women
And I got fond of drink

But I will change my ways now
At this late stage of life
And go home to dear old Ireland
My family and my wife

I will ask God to forgive me
And do the best I can
And I'll put the past behind me
And be a wiser man.

New Age Emigrant

Sinead Maher

A T TWENTY-SEVEN YEARS of age I couldn't claim to have left Ireland's fair shores due to any kind of turmoil – political, economic or personal. I didn't belong to the throngs of people who had fled Ireland to find jobs and opportunity when there were none at home. I left Ireland when the Celtic Tiger was still roaring.

I had just finished my post-graduate diploma in University College Galway and was seeking to move on out into the working world. *The Irish Times* jobs page presented me with an opportunity to work in America; it was waved in front of me like the proverbial carrot, and the temptation to go the USA, in the footsteps of many of my ancestors, drowned out the calls of a job with a Galway company.

So I moved to Alabama, to a company that sponsored my visa. People there looked at me so strangely when they learned I had come over to no one, alone, and was there for the *craic* – I learned that was not accepted lingo there after a little while. Something I was grateful for at every turn was how friendly, charming, funny and open everyone who had gone before me must have been – my Irish predecessors had paved such a welcoming path that I seldom met an unfriendly face.

At home I had always heard that the Irish away from home were more Irish than the Irish themselves. I now understood that I misunderstood this – it's wasn't that people became more Irish, it was that being away from the beauty, character and culture that is Ireland awakens the *Irish* in the soul and makes you want to dance, sing, play your instrument and share all that is home with those around you.

I joke that I went to America to learn to dance. I visited the Gaeltacht twice in my youth and have fond memories of the *céilís* each night and remember going to bed thinking in Irish instead of English. When I hear someone call the 'Walls of Limerick', *Ballai Luimnigh* still rings in my head: *isteach do tri, isteach do tri, amach do tri* . . . And yet I learned to set dance from a fond friend of mine, Mary Dougherty, a native of Washington. Her accent blended with mine so much so that people doubted that she was born and bred in America. She claimed she inherited the lilt in her accent from the many young Irish emigrants who stayed on her grandparents' couch on reaching America.

I have always had enormous pride in being Irish. It seemed that America awakened an awareness that this pride extends beyond my home shores and spreads over all that Irish people had brought there and achieved there.

As a new age emigrant, things were different for me than for most of those who had set foot on those shores before me. My friends and peers now leave Ireland in search of adventure and to see what's out there, knowing that they can return home tomorrow should the feeling take them. Even though transport has shortened travelling time, phone companies competition has ensured ease of calling home and the internet has allowed chatting and e-mails to friends and family, the Atlantic is still as vast as ever it was, and sometimes home seems light years away. I can't begin to comprehend how early emigrants felt knowing they would never return to home, friends and family.

Alabama has become my home away from home. I have great friends and an American family who 'adopted' me two days after my arriving on American soil. America is an immense country, and yet I have good friends in New York, Louisiana, Mississippi, Georgia. The Irish emigration legacy has left a wonderful network of musicians, dancers and, best of all, friends for all us new, unworthy, comfort travellers to benefit from and enjoy.

Never Give Up

Shay McConnon

IN 1848, IRELAND was in the sorrowful grip of the Great Famine, families were being evicted from their homes, and emigration was robbing the country of its sons and daughters. In what became known as the Young Irish Disorders of 1848, the Young Ireland movement led an abortive uprising in Tipperary, resulting in the capture, trial and conviction of nine of its leaders: Pat Donahue, Charles Duffy, Michael Ireland, Morris Lyene, Thomas McGee, Terrence McManus, Thomas Francis Meagher, John Mitchell and Richard O'Gorman.

In the Clonmel courtroom, the charge was treason against the Crown. They were all found guilty, and before passing sentence the judge asked the nine men if they had anything to say. Meagher spoke for them all: 'My Lord, this is our first offence but not our last. If you will be easy with us this once, we promise on our word as gentlemen, to try and do better next time; and next time, we sure won't be fools to get caught.'

Such remarks did nothing to sway the judge towards leniency, and the sentence was that they be hanged, drawn and quartered, '. . . then disposed of as her Majesty shall think fit'. Their future did not look too rosy, but Queen Victoria never got the opportunity to make that decision on their disposal. Following vigorous protestations from around the world, their sentences were commuted to life and transportation. The following year they were shipped to Tasmania.

Transportation did not have the desired effect, however; they did not lie down and give up. Twenty-five years later, in 1874, an astonished Queen Victoria was informed that Sir Charles Duffy, prime minister of Australia, was the same Charles Duffy who had been convicted of treason at that trial in Clonmel! The Queen demanded an investigation, and the results were even more astonishing; some of the Young Irlanders had remained in Australia while others had escaped to America, but all nine had gone on to make their name in high office.

Thomas Francis Meagher was a brigadier in the US army and governor of Montana. Pat Donahue and Terrence McManus were generals in the US army. Morris Lyene became attorney general of Australia and was succeeded in that post by Michael Ireland. Thomas McGee was elected MP for Montreal and later became Canadian minister of agriculture. Richard O'Gorman was governor general of Newfoundland, and John Mitchell was a prominent New York politician before returning to Ireland and completing the circle by being elected MP for Tipperary.

These nine Irishmen proved beyond doubt that although things do not always go the way we would like in life, if we play the cards we are dealt instead of complaining, we can still end up with all the aces.

The Right Road?

Brendan Power

'WHEN YOU COME to a fork in the road, take it.' I love that quote from the former American baseball player Yogi Berra. Like most of his offbeat quotes and sayings, it always makes me laugh, but it also makes me think. My first thought is, 'Did he say it to make us laugh, or did he say it to make us think?' I do not have the answer to that question, but it does make me think, and for me it does have meaning. To me, it means that which direction we take is much less important than the fact that we take some direction. In other words, if we want something to happen, we have to take action, so we have to get on with it and forget about procrastination.

Sometimes, when I am driving and I do come to a fork, I automatically take the road to my planned destination and then start wondering what would have happened if I had gone the other way. 'What would I have seen?' 'Who would I have met?' 'What would the result have been?' Of course, I will never know the answers because I did not go there, but when we feel like a spot of daydreaming, it is an intriguing and interesting way of spending a few minutes.

Thinking further, I believe that Yogi's quote does not just apply to our road journeys. I believe it applies in exactly the same way when we reach a fork, or a crossroads, in our life. Hopefully at that point, instead of just drifting one way or the other, we make a positive decision to take our life in a particular direction, for a particular reason. When that happens, we can always spend a few minutes again wondering about how things would have been if we had gone in the other direction instead.

'If I'd stayed at home instead of emigrating, would I be able to speak Irish?' 'If I'd gone to America instead of staying at home, would my house be on the tourist trail in Hollywood?' 'If I'd trained harder would I have won an All-Ireland medal?' 'If I'd taken that business opportunity, would I be a millionaire?' And so on, and so on, and so on; another wonderful opportunity for daydreaming.

It would be very easy to spend more than just a few minutes lost in those thoughts wondering what the answers are, so just to save you the time, and the trouble, let me tell you the answer. The answer to all those questions, and dozens more, is, 'Maybe.' Maybe I would be famous, or maybe I would be rich, or maybe I would be both. There are lots of *maybes*, but for me there is one definite. Life would definitely not be the same, because if I had taken the other road, I would never have met the beautiful girl who was to become my wife. And that is not the end of it; if we had never married, the world would be a poorer place because our great children would not be here to brighten it up, and that means our wonderful grandchildren would never have been born.

That is not something I want to spend too much time thinking about, so instead I simply thank God that I took the road I did – if I had gone the other way I might have ended up with the money instead.

The Trimogue Banks

Michael O'Grady

As another day is ending, and the sun sinks in the West,
I often think of bygone days, and the place I love best.
My thoughts they take me back there now, I wish I could go
    down
And walk along the Trimogue Banks, in old Kilkelly town.

I often sit and reminisce, of days so long ago,
When we'd sit on the bridge there in the town, and watch the
    waters flow,
The fish they swam in the water clear, leaping up and down,
As we walked along the Trimogue Banks in old Kilkelly
    town.

Kilkelly town is far away, across the ocean blue,
Its sloping street and sandy hills, and its lovely people too.
I wish I could go back today, and it's then I would go down
And walk along the Trimogue Banks in old Kilkelly town.

I long to remember happy days, those bright days of yore,
When we ran through the meadows, and the green fields of
    Culmore.
The old Fair Day, the weighbridge there, there were cattle of
    renown,
And the old Fairgreen along the Trimogue Banks, in old
    Kilkelly town.

Memories come to my mind; it's just like yesterday,
We walked to school in wind and rain, and afterwards did
    play.
And sometimes in the evening, it's then we'd wander down,
And fish along the Trimogue Banks in old Kilkelly town.

That way of life that was back then, has slowly died away,
And people that I knew have died, others old and grey.
At night I think of the cemetery there, as the moon shines
    down,
On the water flowing between the Trimogue Banks in old
    Kilkelly town.

I hope someday I can return, to hear the church bell ring
    once more,
As it calls out from the hillside, across the scenes that I
    adore,
Where I said goodbye to my true love, as we slowly walked
    on down,
We said we'd meet again, on the Trimogue Banks in old
    Kilkelly town.

Crossing Over

Christine Mc Guinness

WHEN I THINK of my mother's family, two things immediately come to mind. They have been fishermen on Lough Neagh for generations, and they have an amazing connection with, and a love for, animals. This love extends to all creatures; while I was growing up one of the most frequently told stories was of my grandmother who saved a rat from certain death by catching it with her fire tongs and carrying it to freedom, safe from the clutches of her two rather large cats.

My Uncle Jim carried on both these traditions. He spent his life fishing for eels on Lough Neagh with his brother Terry, and my own fondest memories is of Jim teaching his Labrador Rasty how to eat from his doggy bowl. This he did by getting down on all fours and showing him by example how this eating business worked.

Each morning as his boat came in to shore, Jim noticed that a beautiful white swan came into the quay. This was quite unusual; swans rarely enter the quay, as it is very busy with boats, nets and activity. The swan became a talking point among the fishermen, and each morning Jim would bring it bread to eat.

Fishermen know that swans mate for life, and the feeling was that perhaps this swan's partner had died and that it would remain alone apart from the flock until its time would come to pass over. Swans hold a very respected place with the fishermen of Ireland, and it is taboo to ever harm them or cause them danger. They not only hold a very important place in our tradition but in all the traditions of the world.

In Greece the swan was sacred to Apollo, god of music, so it was believed that the swan would sing softly at the time of death.

For the Native American Lacota and Dakota peoples, white swan is known as Wohpe; this same Wohpe is known as 'white buffalo calf woman'. So white swan brought the peace pipe, the sacred breath and wisdom, which allowed the native peoples to communicate with Great Spirit and the ancestors. Swan is therefore a messenger of faith.

In our tradition it is held that the white of the swan's feather is the closest thing we get to the white of the angel's wings. It is said that they glide between the worlds, travelling with messages and knowing. Swan represents Samhain in the druidic tradition, and the transition of the soul.

Around about the same time as the appearance of the white swan, Jim and Terry became concerned that they were not catching any fish. Fishermen around them were getting lots, and so they decided to trade places with their neighbours on the lough. Still no eels. The fishermen on Lough Neagh, as in most small fishing communities, are very close-knit and have a strong tradition of helping each other out. They have their own knowing and ways of being. They tried changing the nets, borrowing another's nets, using different bait, and still no eels, while all around good catches were had.

My Uncle Jim died on his boat one morning in early September. Terry, having no other fishermen around and in a state of shock and grief, had the dangerous and hazardous job of steering Jim home to shore. As the boat came in safely, the white swan waited and watched. Terry shouted for help, and eventually someone came who was able to get a doctor, an ambulance and my Aunt Teresa. As Terry waited by the boat, the white swan glided up and after a moment stretched its long white neck into the boat and rested it on Jim's silent chest.

When eventually help did arrive, the swan still remained with its neck across Jim, and because they can be quite dangerous – swans have been known to break a man's arm with its wing or sever a child's fingers with its beak – the swan had to be chased away so that the doctor could get into the boat to confirm that Jim had died.

As the fishermen came to shore that morning, as they saw Jim lie in his boat, the small fishing community now realised why no fish came to the nets of the Conway boat. No fisherman has ever died on Lough Neagh, but the fish knew.

The white swan was never seen again after that morning. Many fishermen looked for it to give it some food, to thank it for the vigil, but none could find it. The crossing over was complete; the sacred white angel bird had held witness to the passing.

Jim's story, the story of his passing, the eels knowing and the white swan's visit are now, I know, part of the folklore of Lough Neagh. Our folklore, stories, traditions, and the traditions of all native peoples on this planet, still hold a truth and wisdom at this time. The animal kingdom rewarded Jim for his care, compassion and love for them by sending their brightest light to be with him on his path.

Our Contributors

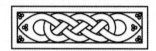

GERRY ADAMS MP, MLA, is the president of Sinn Féin and author of a dozen books, including *Falls Memories* (1982), *Cage Eleven* (1990), *The Street and other stories* (1992), *Before the Dawn* (1996), *An Irish Journal* (2001) and *Hope and History: Making Peace in Ireland* (2003).

MARY ARRIGAN, author and illustrator, has written fourteen teenage novels and sixteen books for younger children. Her books have been translated into six languages. Mary's awards include *The Sunday Times*/CWA Short Story Award, Hennessy Award, and International White Raven Award.

KEN BRUEN studied English in Trinity and has lived and travelled extensively overseas before returning to in his home town of Galway. He has written thirteen published novels, including his internationally celebrated "Jack Taylor" series of dark thrillers set in Galway.

CARI BUZIAK hails from Calgary, Alberta, Canada, where she enjoys creating designs for publication and merchandise. Specialising in Celtic, fantasy and historical art, she uses traditional and digital mediums to create her artwork. You can see her work at www.Aon-Celtic.com.

GAY BYRNE was host of RTÉ's *Late Late Show* for thirty-seven years and of the daily radio show *The Gay Byrne Show* for twenty-seven years. He is now semi-retired, although he does occasional specials for the national broadcaster on both TV and radio; he has also hosted *Who Wants* *to be a Millionaire?* for RTÉ. He lives in County Dublin with his wife Kathleen and has two daughters.

MICHAEL CARRAGHER comes from the border country of south Armagh where he grew up on a farm. He has taught at the University of Arkansas and Louisiana State University, and is at present a teacher of English, history and creative writing in Dublin. His book, *A World Full Of Places,* was published by Blackstaff Press in 1997.

SR CLARE JULIAN is a hermit-sister living as a cloistered contemplative in an isolated hermitage atop a remote Irish mountain. Her work is prayer, and outreach to all, mostly via the internet, for the love of the Lord Jesus Christ. Sister makes rosaries and other craft items and grows flowers and produce. Her web site is www.angelfire.com/ny5/srclarejulian

CON CLUSKEY is the lead singer and voice of The Bachelors, recognised as the best vocal trio of the sixties. Con now spends his time in Yorkshire but often returns to his home in Dublin. Con and his brother Dec, The Bachelors, sing and entertain with their hilarious after dinner speeches and are considered by many to be the most professional act wherever they perform.

MICHAEL COADY lives in County Tipperary. His last book of poetry and prose was entitled *All Souls* (Gallery Press).

ANNE-MARIE COEN is a founder member of the Nenagh Writers' Group and has had work published in the group's own publication and the *Nenagh Guardian.* She has read at the Writers' Centre in Dublin, and both she and her ten-year-old daughter Emma have poetry in *Poems For Lughnasa* and have read their work at Bru Boru, Cashel and the Terryglass Arts Festival.

ULTAN COWLEY has served in the Royal Air Force, obtained a master's at the University College of Wales and lectured in modern history at University College Cork. His latest book is *The Men Who Built Britain.* Ultan is married to the potter Patricia Howard, and they live in County Wexford with their three children, Ruanne, Ben and Tansy.

MICHAEL J. COX was born in Enniskillen but lived in southern Africa for over forty years where he ran a training company and established a reputation as a motivational and inspirational speaker. He has written two books and three video programmes. Michael and his wife, Mary, now live in Dublin.

BILL CULLEN finished school at thirteen and went on to set up what became the biggest Ford dealership in Ireland. He then turned the troubled Renault franchise into a business success story with an annual turnover of over €318 million. He is director of the Irish Youth Foundation and was recipient of the Lord Mayor's Award for instigating the Children's Hour fundraising initiative. *It's a Long Way From Penny Apples* is Bill's autobiography.

CARMEN CULLEN is director of the Oscar Wilde Autumn School in Bray where she now lives. She was a teacher of English for more than twenty years. Her books include *Class Acts, Original Plays for Secondary Schools*, *Sky of Kites, Poetry for Children*, *Under the Eye of the Moon*. She is now working on a diary of wild flower fairy poems. She is involved in a number of residencies.

LESLIE DAWES started her broadcasting career with BBC Radio as a journalist/presenter before moving on to UTV, where she specialised in sport and features. She had her own series *Dawes Explores* and *Province Wide* and says working with a camera team is a wonderful way to tell a story. She now works on feature films and writes comedy material for German, Dutch and Belgian comedy shows.

Journalist ANGELA DOYLE lives and works in County Roscommon. She won the National Media Award for the Provincial Press in 2000, contributed to a collaborative novel in 2001 and edited *Life: A Trip Towards Trust* by motivational speaker Kevin Kelly in 2002. Angela is currently working on a contemporary novel.

GABRIEL FITZMAURICE is a poet, critic and prose writer, in Irish and English. His collections of verse for children have become classics. He is also known as a cultural commentator. Gabriel is a teacher and lives in Kerry with his wife and children.

NANCY FLYNN-McFADDEN is a native of Achill Island, County Mayo. A graduate of University College Galway, she has taught in secondary schools in Mayo, Sligo and Sierra Leone, west Africa. She is now employed by the Western Health Board as Early Years Development Worker, based in Mayo. Widow of the late Dennis McFadden, she has two sons, Rory and Tadhg, and lives in Achill.

RAYMOND FOLEY from Fethard-on-Sea, County Wexford, is one of Ireland's outstanding young illustrators and artists, with an exceptional eye for detail. He spent four years at the School of Art and Design in the city of Limerick, specialising in screen printing, and is currently studying for his master's in interactive media.

MICHAEL FOX followed a career in insurance in England but now lives near Swinford, County Mayo, from where his parents originated. He is further developing his alternate career as a singer, entertainer, recording artiste and broadcaster. Additionally, Michael is a regular contributor of stories relating to Irish heritage, history and rural Ireland to a number of Irish newspapers and journals.

MIRIAM GALLAGHER comes from Waterford. Author, playwright and screenwriter, her work has been published, performed and screened in Ireland, the UK, Europe, the USA and Canada. Her first play, *Fancy Footwork*, was performed at Dublin Theatre Festival, her film, *Gypsies,* was widely screened, and she has had a commissioned play performed at Dublin's Gate Theatre and fiction published in *The Turning Tide*.

FRANCES GAYNOR is a retired nurse who lives in Bagenalstown, County Carlow. She has two brothers who are married and derives great pleasure from music, reading, theatre and travel. She realised one ambition in 2003 with a coach tour through the USA, and her dreams now are to go to India and to have some of her short stories published.

ÁINE GREANEY from County Mayo now lives on Boston's North Shore, where she works as a writer and editor and teaches creative writing. She has published many short stories, essays and features in Irish and American literary journals. Her debut novel, *The Big House,* was published in the UK and Ireland in June 2003. Áine's website is www.AineGreaney.com

MIKE HARDING is a poet, playwright, novelist, travelwriter, film-maker, one-time stand up comedian and traditional Irish banjo player. Born in the North of England, now living on the coast of Connemara writing novels and poems that nobody wants to publish. He is also the world's worst gardener. Plastic flowers die on him.

MARIAN HARKIN is an Independent TD for Sligo/Leitrim. She is a widow with two sons, James and John, and a delightful grandson, Dylan. Marian was previously a maths teacher in Mercy College, Sligo, and has lived in both Manorhamilton, County Leitrim and Sligo Town.

GERARD HARTMANN is a native of Limerick who has developed a reputation for treating many of the world's elite track and field stars. He was physiotherapist to the Irish Olympic team in Atlanta 1996 and the Great Britain Olympic team for Sydney 2000. He also served as physiotherapist to the Great Britain team at the World Athletics Championships.

MOLLY HARVEY is an international speaker, originally from County Waterford and now living in the UK. As a professional keynote speaker, Molly's intention is to give people confidence and the emotional ability to manage change, to enable people to become resilient by encouraging them to be persistent in pursuing success. She has written two books and tapes/CDs, *You Can Do It!* and *The Little Blue Flame.*

YVONNE HEALY is a professional storyteller born in England to Irish parents and raised in the USA. Yvonne travels America entertaining adults and children with the tales she has written and adapted from world mythology, family history and her own experiences. Her CD *Stories from the Heart of the World* from which 'The Healy Cross' is taken, received NAPPA's 2002 Gold Award for Best in Children's Audio.

ROBERT JORDAN is an accountant, trainer and professional speaker, specialising in money matters, motivation and management. Married to Maeve for twenty-nine years, they have two surviving children. They live in Dublin and enjoy frequent visits to their holiday home in County Donegal.

KEVIN KELLY is the author of the best-selling motivation title, *How? When You Don't Know How,* audio *Compelling Communication Strategies* and new book release, *Life – A Trip towards Trust.* Over the past decade he has addressed audiences in the US and Europe on topics such as personal excellence, motivation, communication, sales and leadership.

MARY KENNEDY spent five years as a newscaster and has been co-presenter of the RTÉ daytime show *Open House* since 1999. She presented the Eurovision Song Contest from Dublin in 1995 and presents the annual celebration on the eve of the All-Ireland hurling and football finals, and the People of the Year Awards.

MARY KENNY is a journalist and writer, well known on both sides of the Irish sea. She was born in Dublin, the youngest of four, went to France as a young girl, began her journalistic apprenticeship on the London *Evening Standard,* worked in Ireland where she became a flamboyant founder-member of the Irish Women's Liberation Movement in 1970, and has since lived "between Ireland and England", writing in over twenty publications, most notably the *Irish Independent, Daily Mail, Sunday Telegraph* and *Irish Catholic*. In recent times she has turned her attention to history, and her latest book is a biography of William Joyce, *Lord Haw-Haw*. She is married with two grown-up sons.

SOINBHE LALLY, author and playwright, is the recipient of the prestigious Hennessy Literary Award and was short-listed for the Reading Association of Ireland Children's Books Award and the Bisto Book Award. Her short fiction has appeared on both sides of the Atlantic in such journals as *The Atlantic Monthly* and the *Irish Press*. She lives in Donegal.

SEAN LYONS has worked as a trainer and teacher in Ireland, Africa and Australia. He is an award winning short story writer and essayist and has won many honours as a public speaker, including the British and Irish Humorous Speech Competition in Toastmasters International. Sean is originally from County Mayo and now lives in Kerry with his wife and two children.

SHAY McCONNON was born in Dublin and graduated from UCD. Today he is based in the UK and is a leading international business speaker, author of seventeen books, and his Winning Relationships™ Programme is cascading in many blue chip companies around the world. His latest book, *Resolving Conflict*, has been published in six countries. He is a member of the Magic Circle and uses magic to inspire and entertain his delegates.

RUSS McDEVITT was born in Sligo and brought up in Monaghan. As a young man he set off on a five-year journey around the world. Today Russ is the principal of Empower International in Ontario, Canada, where he lives with his wife Marie.

RANALD MACDONALD travels widely, weaving the magic of stories to children and adults alike. Author of a number of books, he also has a story-based play currently under development by the Abbey Theatre in Dublin. Originally from Edinburgh, he has lived in County Down for a number of years.

VINCENT McDONNELL has published seven novels and over fifty short stories, and has won numerous literary prizes. His novel, *The Broken Commandment*, was described by Graham Greene as 'sad, frightening, merciless and unforgettable', and won a GPA Award in 1989. His latest novel is *Out Of The Flames*. Vincent is married to Joan for thirty years; they have one son and live near Newmarket, County Cork.

ANDY McGOVERN is Ireland's longest survivor of Motor Neurone Disease who, having lost all power in his arms and hands, wrote *They Laughed at this Man's Funeral*, operating the computer with his right foot, each letter or character demanding an individual movement of the toe or heel. Andy says, 'Writing was something I would never have done in my able-bodied days. A disability can oftentimes ignite dormant talents and become the ability to pursue other projects.'

CHRISTINE McGUINNESS may best be described as a dynamic workshop leader, radio presenter and holistic therapist. She works with esoteric traditions through various modalities, including vibrational healing, colour, crystals, angels and the fairy realm. Born in Monaghan, she promotes health and well-being in her health shop Back To Nature in Cavan town.

LIZ McMANUS is TD for County Wicklow and deputy leader of the Labour Party. She is married with four children. Liz enjoys writing to balance her busy political life, and her writing awards include the Hennessy Award, Listowel Short Story Award and the Irish Pen Award.

JOHN MADDEN was born in Ferbane, County Offaly. He spent six years in an orphanage in Kilkenny, followed by three years in an orphanage in Clonmel, County Tipperary. From the age of twelve, he lived in Dublin and at nineteen moved to London. He is now a professional speaker in Kansas.

SINEAD MAHER is from Mullingar, County Westmeath. One of four children, she currently resides in Birmingham, Alabama, where she works as a systems engineer for an engineering company. She plans to stay in the US to experience America and travel for a while, but sees Ireland as the place home will always be and plans to return in the future.

MARTIN MALONE was born in Dublin. His short stories have been published and broadcast widely and have won him The Francis MacManus Award. He was twice short-listed for a Hennessey Award. His novels are *Us*, *After Kafra*, and *The Broken Cedar*. He lives in the Curragh of Kildare.

BRIAN MATTHEWS grew up in New Ross, County Wexford in the 1940s and '50s. He has successfully run his own business systems training company since 1984. This work brought him to the UK, central and eastern Europe and America – North and South. He has a fund of anecdotes and stories to relate, and his work has helped develop his storytelling techniques.

JOE MULLARKEY grew up in Mayo, where he was a keen sportsman. At the age of twenty-two, living in England, he lost both legs in an accident and has learned to walk three times, twice using different types of artificial limbs. Joe, who has recently returned to his native Mayo, is often heard to say, 'Never give up until it's over.'

JOHN EDWARD, 'ED', MURPHY is the founder of the Financial Management Institute, a consulting firm specialising in procurement, finance, public policy, forensic accounting and litigation support. He had a federal career of more than thirty-two years and now lives in Falls Church, Virginia.

AODHÁN Ó CÉILEACHAIR describes himself as 'just an ordinary guy who was born, reared and lives in County

Leitrim and has an interest in how people live their lives – and likes a good cause'.

MICHAEL O'GRADY was born and reared on a small farm in Kilkelly, County Mayo. He lives there with his wife and two children. From an early age he developed a great interest in music and song and has written many songs, most of which, he says, 'are in the attic'. His work has been broadcast on radio and featured in numerous publications.

MAUREEN O'HALLORAN. Originally from Athlone, she moved to Galway to attend a college course in 1982 and decided to stay on afterwards and met her now husband Stephen; they have three children. She is currently studying for a degree in psychology and says she 'enjoys life to the fullest'.

GERRY O'MALLEY qualified as an engineer at UCD. He is now a full time playwright and short story writer; his work has been produced by RTÉ and BBC radio. His stage plays have been performed at the Focus Theatre, Dublin, as well as amateur venues around Ireland, Canada and the USA. He is currently working on a series of monologues for television.

Dr PÁDRAIG PATRIDGE, Dublin-born historian and geographer, living in Germany, has been active in the tourism industry for over fifteen years, firstly for the Irish Tourist Board and since then as a self-employed tourism marketing and public relations consultant. He is a popular speaker on tourism issues and on Celtic and Irish mythology, history and archaeology.

JOHN PERRY was elected to the Dáil at his first attempt in 1997. He is assistant director of organisation and spokesperson on Enterprise, Trade, Employment and Local Development and was formerly junior spokesperson with special responsibility for border issues. John was born in Ballymote, where he lives with his wife, Maire, and son, Jude.

FEARGAL QUINN is executive chairman of Superquinn. For a decade he was chairman of An Post, he chaired a steering committee on the reform of a key element in Ireland's education system and is chairman of the St Patrick's Festival. In 1993 he was elected as an Independent member of the Irish Senate. He has been awarded honorary doctorates by the National Council for Educational Awards and the University of Dublin, and received a papal knighthood in 1994.

LORNA ROBERTS abandoned teaching to become a children's hostess aboard cruise ships. Since leaving the sea she has run a restaurant in Connemara, spending the winter months taking her Irish books to travel agents around Europe. This resulted in her becoming the Irish representative for a Spanish hotel chain – taking Connemara to Spain, and Spain to Ireland.

JOHN SHEAHAN is the fiddle player with the famous Dubliners folk group. In recent years he has made his mark as a composer, his best known piece being 'The Marino Waltz'. He took up writing poetry as a new hobby just two years ago and hopes to publish his first collection in the near future.

PATRICIA SMYTH is a history graduate of Trinity College and a former senior library assistant of Trinity College Library. She is married to George Smyth, a Cavan farmer, and has lived for thirty years in rural Cootehill. In recent years she has worked in the National Library, National Museum and also as a Dublin City Tour Guide.

PATRICK TANSEY is the founder of The Smarter Brain Company, a fast track brain-training organisation. Born and bred in Dublin, he made regular appearances on the long-running British TV show *The Comedians*. He now uses his presentation skills to encourage people to benefit from their brains.

Dr LIAM TWOMEY qualified as a doctor in Trinity College, Dublin, in 1993. He and his wife, Liz O'Sullivan, are general practitioners in Rosslare, County Wexford. In May 2002 he was elected to Dail Eireann as an Independent TD. He is also a contributor to *The Irish Medical News* and other health related journals.

SEÁN WEAFER is an executive coach, trainer, speaker, business author and part-time philosopher. He lives in Dublin with his wife, Sharon, and two small sons, Nicholas and Gregory, who constantly remind him that life should be lived with joy.

CARMEL WYNNE is a trainer, educator, counsellor, writer and broadcaster. She facilitates workshops all over Ireland. A master practitioner in neuro-linguistic programming, qualified life and business coach and motivational speaker. Carmel is the author of *Relationships and Sexuality Education* and *Sex and Young People.* Her latest book is *Coaching: The Key to Achieving Your Goals.*

Laura's Hope

BUYING THIS BOOK does more than provide you with inter-esting and inspirational stories – in our eyes, buying this book makes you a star! Funds from the sale of the book will be used to help Laura's Hope, and the best bit of all is that you are helping people you don't even know and will probably never even get to know.

If Laura were here today, I know she would want to thank you personally, but it's because she is unfortunately not here that the book exists.

Laura's Hope is an international charity, funding research into Huntington's disease, an inherited brain disorder that affects both body and mind. Over its lengthy course, Huntington's disease causes loss of physical control, emotional changes, mental deterioration – and ultimately leads to total incapacitation and death

The fund is named for Laura Evans, who began to show symptoms at the age of thirteen, and eventually died of the less common juvenile form of the disease when she was just twenty-eight years old.

For years it has been common knowledge in the Huntington community that siblings tend to get the disease at about the same age. Scientific research discovered that this is because the nature of the defect in the inherited gene determines either a normal adult onset or the rarer juvenile version.

When Laura was diagnosed in her early teens, the only silver lining in the cloud was that her sister Andrea, who was three years older, did not have it. Andrea was the epitome of a healthy and fit young lady, and proved the point by winning a regional gymnastics championship on the balance beam.

In her mid-twenties Andrea was making plans to marry and decided to confirm once and for all, by means of a recently introduced genetic test, that she did not carry the gene. Against all the odds, the test came back positive, meaning that she carried the lethal gene as well.

Laura's great hope during the last few years of her life was that a treatment would be found before it also claimed her sister. Andrea started to show symptoms of the disease when she was thirty-one.

During most of the fifteen years it took Huntington's to consume Laura, the promise of a cure was off on a distant horizon. Her parents, Warren and Arlene, anxiously watched the research, hoping and praying for a breakthrough. When Laura had gone, they watched and waited until they were confident that a relatively small amount of money (in research terms) could make a real difference. Early in 2001 they realised that time had arrived and founded Laura's Hope.

Thank you for your support by buying this book.

'May you live all the days of your life.'
Jonathan Swift

The Books of Alice Taylor – *a selection*

To School Through the Fields

"One of the most richly evocative and moving portraits of childhood [ever] written ... A journey every reader will treasure and will want to read over and over again." *Boston Herald*
ISBN 086322 099 1; 184 pages;
198 x 129mm; Paperback Memoir
Rights: world except North America, Germany, Poland, Japan, Netherlands, Slovakia, Audio, Large Print

Quench the Lamp

Taylor describes the past vividly and without complaint as years of hard labor for herself, parents and siblings, making clear that the days also were full of fun shared with neighbors in the close-knit community." *Publishers Weekly*
ISBN 086322 112 2; 190 pages;
198 x 129mm; Paperback Memoir
Rights: world except North America, Germany, Poland, Japan, Audio, Large Print

The Village

"What makes the story unique is Taylor's disarming style; she writes as though she were sitting next to you, at dusk, recounting the events of her week... Taylor has a knack for finding the universal truth in daily details." *Los Angeles Times*

ISBN 086322 142 4; 184 pages;
198 x 129mm; Paperback Memoir
Rights: world except North America, Germany, Poland, Japan, Audio, Large Print

Country Days

"A rich patchwork of tales and reminiscences by the bestselling village postmistress from Co. Cork. Alice Taylor is a natural writer." *Daily Telegraph*
ISBN 086322 168 8; 192 pages;
198 x 129mm; Paperback Memoir
Rights: world except North America, Germany, Poland, Japan, Audio, Large Print

The Woman of the House

"This well-crafted novel explores the mixed fortunes of the residents in an Irish village. Taylor skilfully shows the intricacies of country life and the strong tide of emotions which flows under the most placid of exteriors." *Belfast Telegraph*
"An entrancing story written with much sensitivity and great depth of feeling, this is a delightful read." *Booklist*
ISBN 086322 249 8; 310 pages; 198 x 129mm; Paperback Fiction
Rights: world except North America, Germany, Large Print and Audio

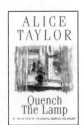

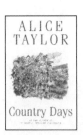
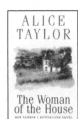

The Books of Gerry Adams – *a selection*

Before the Dawn: An Autobiography

"One of the most controversial but important political memoirs of recent times." *Publishing News*

"A definitive history of the Irish struggles of the 1970s, from the nationalist point of view. Adams, a fine writer, presents a straightforward, unapologetic memoir." *Publisher's Weekly*

"His style is graceful; he has a keen eye for detail and a good grasp of dialogue." *Time*

ISBN 0 86322 289 7; 348 pages; 198 x 129mm; Paperback Memoir

Rights: world except North America

Cage Eleven

"Quite brilliant... a tribute to a particular kind of survival by a group of people who have committed their lives to a deeply-held political belief about their country." *Books Ireland*

"He is a natural storyteller, with a warm and agile wit... The writing is natural and, one might say, writerly." *Listener*

"Evocative and often witty cameos of prison life... This is an important book for understanding the strength of [Irish Republican] tradition." *Times Literary Supplement*

ISBN 0 86322 292 7 156 pages; 198 x 129mm; Paperback Memoir

Rights: world except North America

The Street and other stories

"About all the stories there is a certain elegiac quality: a sense that something important is slipping away, being lost... The warmth of Adams's writing comes from the affection of a man for the remembered things of his past... *The Street* demonstrates that Adams can write well." *Times Literary Supplement*

ISBN 0 86322 293 5; 156 pages; 198 x 129mm; Paperback Fiction

Rights: world except North America

An Irish Journal

"Make no mistake, Adams is a talented and engaging writer... [His] eclectic approach is highly refreshing and serves to remind us that, despite his obvious preoccupation with the day-to-day minutiae of dealings with those involved in the peace process, his concerns and aspirations are not limited to this alone. Peace and social justice for others, family, friendship and, wherever possible, relaxation are equally important." *Irish Democrat*

ISBN 0 86322 282 X; 288 pages; 216 x 135mm; Paperback Original Current Affairs

Rights: world

The Books of Walter Macken – *a selection*

Rain on the Wind

"A raw, savage story full of passion and drama set amongst the Galway fishing community." *Irish Independent*

ISBN 0 86322 185 8;
320 pages; Paperback Fiction
Rights: World, except France, Germany

The Green Hills

His short stories, which he described as "dreams on paper", bring to life a richly varied cast of characters, and in all he writes with a unique feeling for the lives of the ordinary people.

ISBN 0 86322 216 1; 216 pages; Paperback Fiction
Rights: World

The Bogman

"Comic and touching by turn; the anecdotes glide as smoothly as summer streams; the farming scenes are vividly done; it is all skilfully told with excellent dramatic moments." *Spectator*

ISBN 0 86322 184 X; 320 pages;
Paperback Fiction
Rights: World, except Germany

City of the Tribes

"Full of insight and humour, they celebrate the qualities of ordinary people in their struggles with poverty in and around Galway in the 1940s." *Woman's Way*

ISBN 0 86322 276 5;
244 pages; Paperback Fiction
Rights: World

God Made Sunday

"Instead of throwing together these reprints from splodgy old type with any old cover, Brandon have redesigned and reset the series with care and great respect." *Books Ireland*

ISBN 0 86322 217 X;
222 pages; Paperback Fiction
Rights: World, except France

Sunset on the Window-Panes

"In his company, to use a fine phrase of Yeats, brightness falls from the air." *Newcastle Chronicle*

ISBN 0 86322 254 4;
284 pages; Paperback Fiction

Rights: World

The Jack Taylor Novels by Ken Bruen

Ken Bruen

"Outstanding... Ireland's version of Scotland's Ian Rankin... Bruen has a rich and mordant writing style, full of offbeat humor. Perhaps the standard bearer for a new subgenre called 'Hibernian Noir'." *Publishers Weekly*

"Blurring different stylistic and genre traits is not only necessary for fiction to evolve and remain relevant, but it also makes for a damn exciting read... [Bruen's] books are like odd architectural wonders, stark, strangely unsettling, beautifully classical, yet wholly modern." *Crime Factory*

The Guards

"Edgy, pitch-black humour... With few, if any, antecedents *The Guards* is one of the curiously rare Irish crime novels, and the first set in Bruen's home town of Galway." *Guardian*

"Hard-boiled, eccentric, darkly comic: Bruen bows to but doesn't just mimic James M. Cain and the other great noirists in a breakout novel not to be missed." *Kirkus Reviews*

"Crime book of the year... Gripping, brutal and very funny." *The Age*

ISBN 0 86322 323 0; 304 pages; 198 x 129mm; Paperback; New edition May 2004

Rights: world except North America, Australia and New Zealand, France, Italy, Russia, Netherlands, Albania

The Killing of the Tinkers

"Jack Taylor is back in town, weighed down with wisecracks and cocaine... Somebody is murdering young male travellers and Taylor, with his reputation as an outsider, is the man they want to get to the root of things... Compulsive... rapid fire... entertaining." *Sunday Tribune*

"Fast moving and immensely readable." *BookView Ireland*

ISBN 0 86322 294 3; 308 pages; 198 x 129mm; Paperback Original

Rights: world except North America, Australia and New Zealand, France, Italy, Russia, Netherlands, Albania

The Magdalen Martyrs

"The prolific Bruen is breaking in a big way in the US, and his time has come. This is Irish noir with humour and guts." *Crime Bookseller*

Jack Taylor, traumatised, bitter and hurting from his last case, has resolved to give up the finding business. However, he owes the local hard man a debt of honour and it appears easy enough: find "the Angel of the Magdalen" – a woman who helped the unfortunates incarcerated in the infamous laundry.

ISBN 0 86322 302 8; 308 pages; 198 X 129mm; Paperback Original

Rights: World except North America, Australia and New Zealand

Recently Published Non-Fiction

America Rules
Tom Hanahoe

The disturbing, definitive account of globalization and the new American imperialism. This unique and compelling book tells the story of the rise of the United States and the world's largest corporations to a position of near-global joint domination. It shows how the lives of Americans and the affairs of their country are controlled by a small elite ruling class drawn from the corporate sector which has sacrificed the rights, the needs and the lives of many of the world's people to US corporate greed.

ISBN 0 86322 309 5; 288 pages; 216 x 135mm; Paperback Original Current Affairs

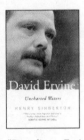

David Ervine: Uncharted Waters
Henry Sinnerton

"There is not a more impressive politician in Northern Ireland than David Ervine." *Senator George Mitchell*

"Revealing... Ervine is an impressive advocate of modern unionism." *Irish Examiner*

"Sinnerton is strong on explaining recent history from a loyalist political perspective... David Ervine played a key role in delivering the loyalist ceasefire. He negotiated directly with Albert Reynolds... He humanised unionism... He stopped Mo Mowlam undermining the consent principle. He did all this under fire from mainstream unionism and under a very real IRA death threat." *Fortnight*

ISBN 0 86322 312 5; 256 pages; 198 X 129mm; Paperback Biography

A Touchstone for the Tradition
Tony Kearns and Barry Taylor

Since 1973 Miltown Malbay has become, for one week in early July, the traditional music capital of the world. The crowded main street echoes with a plethora of languages and dialects, the bars are full to bursting point, and the sounds of jigs, reels and hornpipes fill the summer air. *A Touchstone for the Tradition* is an evocation in pictures and words of this remarkable community of Irish music enthusiasts, drawn together by the urge to learn music, to play music, to dance, to teach and to listen.

"Succeeds admirably in describing the ongoing success of the Willie Clancy Summer School... There's beauty on almost every page." *Irish Examiner*

ISBN 0 86322 308 7; 160 pages; 246 x 189mm; Paperback Music/Photography

Recently Published Fiction

Skin of Dreams
Evelyn Conlon

Fiction with a sharp documentary edge: the story, set in Ireland and the US, of one woman's encounter with murder, justice and execution.

"A courageous, intensely imagined and tightly focused book that asks powerful questions of authority... this is the kind of Irish novel that is all too rare." Joseph O'Connor

"She is one of Ireland's major truly creative writers." *Books Ireland*

"Through two continents and two generations Evelyn Conlon traces the countenance of life and death and its so-called punishment, in a tale deftly told with revelation that startles with new insight." Sam Reese Sheppard, co-author of *Mockery of Justice*

ISBN 0 86322 306 0; 232 pages; 216 x 135mm; Paperback Original Fiction

Rights: world

The Land where Stories End
David Foster

"Stunningly produced...utterly original. A post-modern fable which explores male sexuality, myth, alchemy and the hermetic tradition." *Irish Examiner*

"A worthy successor to Flann O'Brien." *Guardian*

"Foster's prose is as funny as an overturned lorryload of laughing gas – and equally disabling." *Yorkshire Post*

"A wonderful mixture of the satiric and the visionary, or of the scabrous and the near-lyrical, that I find exhilirating." *Sydney Morning Herald*

"One of Australia's boldest and most inventive novelists." *The Age*

"Foster possesses a keen eye for human folly, the ability to hijack his audience, and a readiness to be mordant and merciless while retaining an unrelenting hold over his readers." *Australian Book Review*

ISBN 0 86322 311 7; 224 pages; 198 x 129mm; Hardback Fiction

Rights: world except Australia and New Zealand (Duffy & Snellgrove)

Testimony of an Irish Slave Girl
Kate McCafferty

The searing story of a young girl kidnapped from her home in Galway and shipped out to Barbados.

"McCafferty's haunting novel chronicles an overlooked chapter in the annals of human slavery... A meticulously researched piece of historical fiction that will keep readers both horrified and mesmerized." *Booklist*

"A harrowing tale about events too long ignored by textbooks." *Los Angeles Times*

"Enlightening not only from a historical standpoint, but also from its psychological insights on the relationship between slaves and their owners." *St. Louis Post-Dispatch*

"McCafferty does a remarkably vivid and thorough job of portraying what life was like for the indentured Irish." *Boston Globe*

ISBN 0 86322 314 1; 224 pages; 216 x 138mm; Hardback Fiction

Rights: Britain and Ireland; other rights Viking USA